The Little
Synology DSM

Nicholas Rushton, BA Hons.
Callisto Technology And Consultancy Services
Second Edition © 2018

Table of Contents

1 PREPARATION   9

1.1 CHOOSING A DISKSTATION   9
1.2 HARD DRIVES   10
1.3 RAID   12
1.4 LOCATION   15
1.5 ELECTRICAL CONSIDERATIONS   15
1.6 COMPUTERS AND DEVICES   16
1.7 INFRASTRUCTURE   16

2 INSTALLATION OF DSM   19

2.1 INSTALLATION USING WEB ASSISTANT   20
2.2 FIVE MINUTE TOUR OF DISKSTATION MANAGER   26
2.3 CONFIGURE NETWORKING   30
2.4 POWER MANAGEMENT   32
2.5 FILE SERVICES   35
2.6 OVERVIEW OF STORAGE IN DSM   38
2.7 QUICKCONNECT: THE KEY TO REMOTE CONNECTIVITY   40

3 SHARED FOLDERS   42

3.1 CREATING A SHARED FOLDER   42
3.2 ENABLING HOME FOLDERS   45
3.3 DELETING OR CHANGING A SHARED FOLDER   47

4 USERS   48

4.1 NAMING CONVENTIONS   48
4.2 CREATING A USER   49
4.3 MODIFYING, DELETING AND COPYING USERS   53

5 ACCESSING THE DISKSTATION   54

5.1 USING A BROWSER   54
5.2 USING WINDOWS EXPLORER/FILE EXPLORER   56
5.3 ACCESSING SHARED FOLDERS USING THE RUN COMMAND   57
5.4 MAPPING DRIVES MANUALLY   58
5.5 USING SYNOLOGY ASSISTANT   61
5.6 CONNECTING MACS   65
5.7 SMARTPHONES & TABLETS   67

5.8 CONNECTING LINUX COMPUTERS 68

6 SYNOLOGY DRIVE & OFFICE 70

6.1 OVERVIEW OF SYNOLOGY DRIVE 70
6.2 INSTALLING & CONFIGURING SYNOLOGY DRIVE & OFFICE 71
6.3 ACCESSING DRIVE WITH A BROWSER 73
6.4 DESKTOP DRIVE CLIENT 75
6.5 MOBILE DRIVE CLIENT 78
6.6 USING OFFICE 80

7 BACKUPS 82

7.1 BACKING UP THE DISKSTATION TO AN EXTERNAL DRIVE 84
7.2 RESTORING FILES FROM A BACKUP 92
7.3 BACKING UP USING CLOUD SERVICES 94
7.4 BACKING UP COMPUTERS TO THE DISKSTATION 98
7.5 CLOUD STATION BACKUP 99
7.6 BACKING UP MACS USING TIME MACHINE 102

8 MULTIMEDIA & STREAMING 104

8.1 MEDIA SERVER ("DLNA") 104
8.2 MEDIA INDEXING 108
8.3 MOMENTS 110
8.4 OTHER SYNOLOGY MULTIMEDIA APPLICATIONS 115

9 MISCELLANEOUS TOPICS 116

9.1 PACKAGE CENTER 116
9.2 SECURITY ADVISOR 120
9.3 ANTIVIRUS ESSENTIAL 121
9.4 PASSWORD SETTINGS 123
9.5 MANUALLY CHECKING THE DISKSTATION USING WIDGETS 125
9.6 CHECKING THE HEALTH OF THE DISKS 126
9.7 CHECKING FOR DSM UPDATES 128
9.8 SUPPORT CENTER 130
9.9 PRINTING 131
9.10 PERSONALIZING THE DESKTOP 133
9.11 RESETTING THE ADMIN PASSWORD IF LOST 134
9.12 PREPARING THE DISKSTATION FOR DISPOSAL 135

COMMENTS & REVIEWS FROM OTHER PURCHASERS

You are in good company - thousands of people have purchased guides from CTACS to help them setup their home and business networks. This is what purchasers of our Synology Guides have written in their reviews:

"I set up my Synology without the help of this book only to realize it was not doing what I wanted it to do. I bought the book, read through it page by page. Eventually, I realized I had to start over and reset my disk station to factory setting and then walk through the set up using this book. It made it simple and helped me understand the process better. Until I got this book my disk station was worthless to me because of my misunderstanding of how it all works together." – DK. Feb 2018

"I have familiarity with most computers in general. But when I got my 1st NAS device, I decided it couldn't hurt to have some hands-on advice. Nick Rushton's book on setting up my Synology NAS has been the best spent money and has helped me get up and running in a small amount of time. No nonsense, easily understood step-by-step recommendations were what I needed. I highly recommend his guide." – G, Jan 2017

"This is about as good as it gets for Synology NAS owners and tries to be a plain English guide to a very technical subject. Shame Synology couldn't include something similar with their NAS". – EB, Mar 2017

"Oh man, wished I had this to start with" – MO, Dec 2016

"Does everything it says on the tin. You really need one of these." – RT, Dec 2014

"Simple, concise and no-nonsense guide to setting up NAS in the comfort of your home. Much better than Synology Help website." – AI, May 2016

"This should come with DSM! Well written and concise. Just what a new user would need to get going and get the most out of the Synology system." – GL, July 2015

"Five Stars. Excellent book, should be included with the NAS". – Amazon Customer, Oct 2015

"Extremely useful guide to setting up the Synology NAS system. It is written in a user friendly, non-technical way and the author makes numerous recommendations to assist newcomers in making set up decisions. Very worthwhile and highly recommended if you're not exactly sure of what you are dealing with". – MB, Oct 2014

"Made setting up the Synology NAS server super simple. Walks you thru all the common stuff step by step. Great help. Thanks." – L, Jan 2015

"The perfect companion while setting up a Synology NAS. This book explains everything thing worth knowing when setting up a Synology NAS. It gives self-confidence to a non-professional IT person and makes the setup of a Synology NAS really smooth and enjoyable. Thanks a lot for good tips and tricks on maintenance and daily usage. Well written and up to date". – MS, Jan 2016

"Great guide to do initial set-up of Synology NAS . Clear step by step instructions. Good value for money!" – HLB, June 2015

INTRODUCTION

If you are reading this, then chances are you already know what Network Attached Storage (NAS) is and may have purchased or are about to purchase a Synology NAS unit. But for those who do not, or by way of recap, it consists of a large amount of disk storage contained in its own box. Unlike most external hard drives, which connect to a single computer using a USB cable, a NAS connects to a router or network switch using an Ethernet cable and this enables it to be accessed and shared by computers and other devices on the local network. In addition, the NAS is intelligent - you can think of it as a small computer but without its own screen, keyboard and mouse - and this enables it to optionally run apps that provide additional capabilities. An alternative name for a NAS box is *server*, and we will tend to use this term as well in this book.

So, what can a NAS do? Many things. Some popular uses are:
- To provide extra storage for computers
- To be a backup system for computers
- To provide a shared, common area where a business or family can store their documents and other files
- To act as a central library for music, photos and videos, along with the ability to stream them to computers, tablets and smartphones
- To act as a private 'cloud' system, providing controlled remote access to your data similar to Dropbox or Google Drive, but totally under your own control and with effectively unlimited usage plus no subscription charges

With superb functionality and ease of use through the acclaimed DSM operating system, Synology DiskStations are the NAS devices of choice for the discerning purchaser: they can do all of the above things with aplomb. But this power and flexibility comes at a price and setting up a DiskStation for the very first time can seem a daunting prospect for someone who has not done so before.

This guide, based around the current version of DSM and with plenty of illustrations, easy-to-follow instructions and based on years of real-world experience, will take you through it from start to finish and help ensure that your network is a success. It is a streamlined or 'lite' version of the popular and highly regarded CTACS *Synology NAS Setup Guide for Home & Small Business*, with some of the more advanced topics removed. If you just want to be up and running as quickly as possible, this guide is for you. If you require more information or are an advanced or business user, you will probably prefer the full version.

The guide progresses in a logical order. Chapter 1 is concerned with preparation and provides some useful background information about buying and preparing a DiskStation. Chapter 2 covers the initial installation of DSM and customizing the hardware options of the DiskStation. Chapter 3 describes how to create shared folders and Chapter 4 discusses the creation of users and groups. Chapter 5 covers the various methods for connecting PCs and Macs to the DiskStation in order to access data. Chapter 6 is about setting up your own personal cloud, using *Synology Drive*. Chapter 7 is all about backups, whilst Chapter 8 introduces the multimedia and streaming options available in DSM. Finally, Chapter 9 discusses miscellaneous and housekeeping topics to help you get more out of your DiskStation and keep it in good health.

In a hurry? The first five chapters will get you up and running ASAP. Then return and explore at leisure.

1 PREPARATION

1.1 Choosing a DiskStation

Synology offer many different models of their NAS hardware, designed to cater for everyone from home users through to the largest of enterprises. The models vary according to form factor, number of hard drives that can be used, performance and price:

Form Factor – DiskStations are standalone units designed to sit on top of a cupboard or desk; *RackStations* are designed to be mounted in standard computer cabinets (racks) that take devices that are 19" (48cm) wide. Home and small business users will typically use DiskStations, but some businesses may have a cabinet, perhaps to hold other equipment as well, in which case a RackStation may be a more convenient choice. In this guide, the generic term 'DiskStation' is generally used but this should be read to mean any NAS unit from Synology as they are the same thing other than in form factor.

Number of Hard Drives – Synology NAS units can hold between 1 and 24 hard drives, depending on the model. Having more drives allows more storage capacity and permits the use of RAID - discussed shortly - to improve resilience and throughput.

Performance - Some DiskStations and RackStations have more powerful processors, more memory (RAM) and are equipped with multiple network adaptors. These are typically aimed at business users or home users with more demanding requirements.

Synology have a logical naming convention for the DiskStations – they are generally called *DSdyy* where *d* is the number of drive bays and *yy* is the year that the model was released (correspondingly, RackStations are named *RSdyy*). Many of them have a suffix, for instance the letter *j* indicates that it is a lower price version of another model whereas a plus sign signifies a more powerful variant. For instance, the DS218+ is an enhanced model with two drive bays, released in 2018.

Choosing the right model can be confusing as there is some overlap between them, but in general you want to buy the most capable one you can afford. If you have or are planning to have large amounts of data, consider buying a model with more than two drive bays.

1.2 Hard Drives

DiskStations are not supplied by Synology with hard drives already installed in them. Rather, the idea is that the customer buys the drives separately and installs them, which is quite easy to do, else buys a ready-populated unit from a reseller. This approach is generally better because it offers more choice. Synology NAS units are very flexible in terms of the brand and type of hard drives that can be used in them. It is not necessarily the case that any drive or combination of drives can be installed, although all popular ones can and there is a list of supported drives that can be found on the Synology website.

Hard drives are generally manufactured in 3.5" (8.9cm) and 2.5" (6.4cm) form factors and most DiskStations can use either, although some DiskStations require adaptor brackets to use the 2.5" ones (an exception to this is the DS Slim series, which is specifically designed to use 2.5" drives only). 3.5" drives offer higher capacities and better price performance but 2.5" drives use less power, generate less vibration, are generally quieter in operation and are increasingly becoming a popular choice.

It is recommended to buy drives that have been designed for use in NAS such as the Western Digital Red series, Toshiba N300 or Seagate IronWolf (the latter has specific support within DSM). These NAS drives are typically rated for use in systems with up to 8 bays; for larger models, 'Pro' versions are available and recommended. For systems with more than one drive, it is preferable that all the drives are the same model and capacity, although not a prerequisite.

Although most of today's hard drives are mechanical, solid state drives based around flash memory and known as SSDs are increasingly being seen in laptop computers and elsewhere and will probably become the norm in all computing devices. At present, they are considerably more expensive than their mechanical counterparts for the high-capacity ones that would be of most use in NAS. The popular brands are supported by Synology; however, the main benefits are reduced power consumption and the absence of noise, rather than any performance improvements in typical usage. However, on some DiskStations, SSDs can be configured for caching, which does boost overall system performance. So called hybrid or SSHD drives, which combine a conventional mechanical platter with some solid state memory, do not offer any particular benefits in a NAS system.

1.3 RAID

RAID is short for *Redundant Array of Independent (or Inexpensive) Disks*. There are various types of RAID, referred to using a numbering system: RAID 0, RAID 1, RAID 5 and so on. The basic idea is to improve reliability and performance by using multiple disks to provide redundancy and share the workload. Synology support many different RAID levels, depending on the model and the physical drives installed, but the most common scenarios in home and small business systems are RAID 0, RAID 1, RAID 5, RAID 6, SHR and JBOD. If you have a DiskStation that uses a single hard drive then this section is not applicable to you and you can skip it.

RAID 0 consists of two identical drives. When data is written, some goes on one drive and some goes on the other. As both drives are being written to or read simultaneously, throughput is maximised. However, as bits of files are scattered across the two drives, if one drive fails then everything is lost. Also, the speed of disk drives is not typically the bottleneck in many NAS systems. For these reasons RAID 0 should generally be avoided (strictly speaking, it is not a RAID system at all).

RAID 1 consists of two identical drives that mirror each other. When a file is saved there are actually two separate but identical copies behind the scenes, one held on each drive, even though you can only see one as the mirroring process itself is invisible. If one of the drives fails, the second one automatically takes over and the system carries on without interruption. At the earliest opportunity the faulty drive should be replaced with a new one; the system is then synced so it becomes a true copy of the remaining healthy drive in a process known as 'rebuilding the array'.

In a RAID 1 system, the total usable storage capacity is half that of the total drive capacity installed. For example, if a DiskStation has two 2TB drives installed then the total amount of usable storage capacity is 2TB rather than 4TB.

RAID 5 uses at least three but preferably four drives. Data is written simultaneously across all the drives, along with what is known as parity information. The benefit of this is that the system can cope with the failure of any one single drive. RAID 5 is considered to offer a good combination of price, performance and resilience. Whereas a RAID 1 system loses 50% of the total drive capacity in order to provide resilience, RAID 5 typically loses only about 25%. For instance, if a DiskStation has four 2TB drives installed then the total amount of usable storage capacity is 6TB rather than 8TB.

RAID 6 uses at least four but preferably five or more drives. It is similar to RAID 5, but uses two sets of parity information written across the drives. The added benefit of this approach is that the system can cope with the simultaneous failure of two of the drives, thereby making it more resilient than RAID 5, but it loses more capacity in order to provide that resilience. There may also be a performance hit compared with RAID 5 due to the additional parity processing. If a server has five 2TB drives installed in a RAID configuration, then the total amount of usable storage capacity is 6TB rather than 10TB.

SHR and SHR-2 (Synology Hybrid Raid) is a more flexible approach to RAID, developed by Synology. Whereas conventional RAID systems require multiple drives of identical capacity, SHR can work with drives of differing capacities. It creates a mixture of usable space plus puts some aside for redundant storage, described as 'protection' by Synology.

SHR is of particular relevance when there is a mixture of different capacity drives, plus is easier to expand by adding further drives at a later points. It also avoids the need for any technical knowledge of what is going on behind the scenes for non-technical users as 'it just works'. SHR is Synology's preferred system and is installed by default during most installations of DSM.

In simple terms, SHR and SHR-2 can be considered as analogous to RAID 5 and RAID 6 respectively. By way of example, if you had a pair of 2TB drives, a 1TB one and a 500GB one then SHR would give 3.5TB of usable space and use a further 2TB for protection.

JBOD stands for *Just a Bunch of Disks* and is not actually a RAID system at all. Rather, it aggregates all the drives together to create one large volume that provides the maximum amount of storage space, but without any protection. For example, with the same drives as in the previous example you would get the full 5.5TB storage with JBOD rather than just 3.5TB storage as with SHR.

What to do? If you have a DiskStation with a single drive, then the question of RAID does not arise. If you have a DiskStation with two drive bays, then you can use RAID 1 or SHR if data protection is most important to you or use JBOD if you need the maximum amount of space. If you have a DiskStation with four drive bays, it can be configured as RAID 5 or SHR if protection is most important or JBOD if you need the maximum amount of space. If you have a DiskStation with five or more drives, it can be configured as RAID 6 or SHR-2 if protection is most important or JBOD if you need the maximum amount of space. However, during the installation of DSM, it will make a decision for you based upon the number of drives it finds and most people won't need to do anything at all.

One important thing to note is that a RAID system is **not** a backup system. It can help prevent data loss in the event of problems, but it is still important to make separate provision for backup. For instance, if the DiskStation was stolen or the premises went up in flames, then the data would be lost regardless of whether and whatever RAID system was used.

1.4 Location

DiskStations are fairly rugged, but as with any electrical apparatus some thought needs to be given to the location. They should be placed away from direct sunlight and any source of heat, such as a radiator. Avoid locations that are wet or damp. As little physical access is required the unit can be located out of sight and reach, for instance in a cupboard or a locked room or otherwise out of reach. Most models generate very little noise and can usually be operated in an office or family room without too much disruption. Preferably, the DiskStation should be connected directly to the router using a wired Ethernet connection.

1.5 Electrical Considerations

It is possible that data loss can occur if the mains electrical power fails unexpectedly whilst the DiskStation is running. The best way to mitigate against this is to use an intelligent UPS (Uninterruptible Power Supply) with the DiskStation; in the event of power problems this will enable it to continue operating for short periods and to then shut down in an orderly manner if necessary. Most popular brands work with Synology and a full list of supported UPS's can be found on the Synology website. In a business environment, the use of an UPS should be considered mandatory.

If a UPS is not used - which is usually the case in a domestic environment - then the DiskStation should at least be connected to a clean electrical power supply via a surge protector.

1.6 Computers and Devices

Just about any modern computer can be used with a DiskStation. The computers can be running any mixture of Windows 10, Windows 8/8.1, Windows 7, Windows Vista or Windows XP. Home or Professional versions of Windows are equally suitable. Apple Macintosh computers running most versions of the Mac OS can be connected, as can Linux PCs (although the latter are not specifically discussed in this guide). Devices running iOS (iPad, iPhone), Android (tablets and Smartphones) or Windows Phone can be connected, as can many smart televisions and gaming boxes. However, Chromebooks can only be connected in a relatively limited sense.

1.7 Infrastructure

The term *infrastructure* is used here to describe the physical network, basically the boxes and wires that connect everything together and to the outside world. The difference between a home setup and a business setup tends to be one of scale, but the equipment and principles are largely the same.

In a home setup, a device called a combined wireless router is commonly used. This connects to the internet, which may be a cable, fibre, satellite or ADSL service, directly or possibly via a separate box (commonly referred to, albeit incorrectly, as a modem). It has wireless capabilities for linking laptops, tablets and smartphones. There will be several Ethernet ports, used for connected wired devices such as desktop PCs. The NAS box needs to be wired directly to one of these ports.

A small business may be linked to the internet via cable, fibre, satellite or ADSL, or may even have its own leased line connection, perhaps using a router. The router may be integrated with or be connected to a separate firewall. In turn this connects to a network switch, to which the NAS should be connected using an Ethernet cable. Desktop PCs, printers and wireless access points (WAPs) are wired into the switch; depending on the amount of kit and layout of the office there may be one or more additional switches also connected.

The above descriptions are generic but should bear some resemblance to your infrastructure. Some key points are:

- The NAS should be connected to the main network switch or combined wireless router using an Ethernet cable.
- Use wired connections whenever possible as performance is so much better than wireless. Wired devices should be of Gigabit specification (some DiskStations also support 10 Gigabit Ethernet).
- For wireless devices such as laptops and tablets, make sure they operate at 801.11n or 801.11ac standards.
- Check the specification of the combined wireless router if you are using one. Many ISPs (Internet Service Providers) supply relatively low-cost models, often free of charge when you sign-up with them. These can be of average quality, for instance the Ethernet ports may not be Gigabit or the latest wireless standards may not be supported. Spending money on professional or prosumer ("professional consumer") routers and switches will usually give better performance and reliability.

Typical Home or
Small Business
Infrastructure

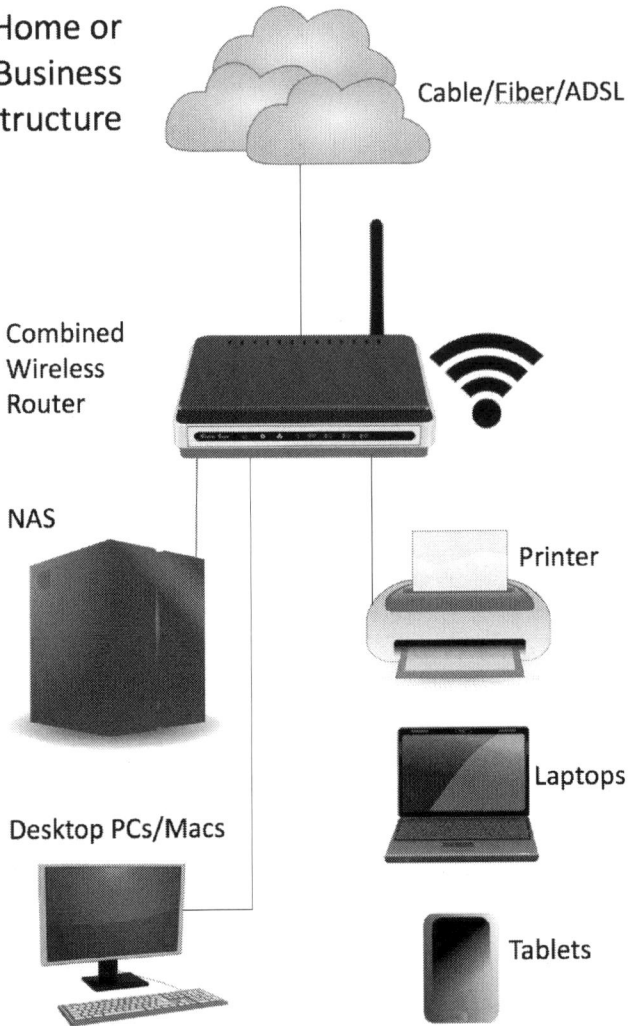

Cable/Fiber/ADSL

Combined
Wireless
Router

NAS

Printer

Desktop PCs/Macs

Laptops

Tablets

Figure 1: Typical Networking Infrastructure

2 INSTALLATION OF DSM

DiskStation Manager or DSM, the operating system or firmware, is the key thing that differentiates Synology from all the other brands of Network Attached Storage. It has such familiar features as a Desktop, taskbar and a drag-and-drop interface, analogous to what people are accustomed to with Windows, Mac and Linux PCs. Other NAS vendors have been playing catch-up, but with the latest version Synology have once again pushed ahead of the pack in the opinion of many people.

The assumption in this chapter is that you are installing a brand new DiskStation. If this is not the case – maybe you have obtained a previously used model, for instance – you might find it helpful to first take a quick look at sections **9.11 Resetting the Admin Password if Lost** and **9.12 Preparing the DiskStation for Disposal**.

Commence by physically installing the hard drive(s); how to do this varies by model but is described in the getting started leaflet supplied with the DiskStation. Having done so, connect it to the network using an Ethernet cable (if the DiskStation has multiple network adaptors, connect only one of them). You can then install DSM using *Web Assistant*: all you need is a device with a browser, such as a computer or an iPad. You access a special website, answer a few simple questions and it does most of the hard work for you. Synology suggest using Firefox or Chrome, but in practice Internet Explorer and Safari seem to work just as well. Synology also have an app – *DS Finder* – available for iOS and Android tablets and smartphones. This mirrors Web Assistant can do much of the initial installation, although it will still be necessary to use a conventional browser at some stage to finalise the configuration.

2.1 Installation Using Web Assistant

Web Assistant is invoked by typing the following address into the browser on a computer or other device connected to the same local network: *find.synology.com*. After scanning your network for a few seconds it should find the DiskStation and display the following screen. Note: if you receive a message from the browser about having to enable intranet settings, do so. Also, if you have a DiskStation with multiple network adapters, make sure that only the first one is connected when using Web Assistant.

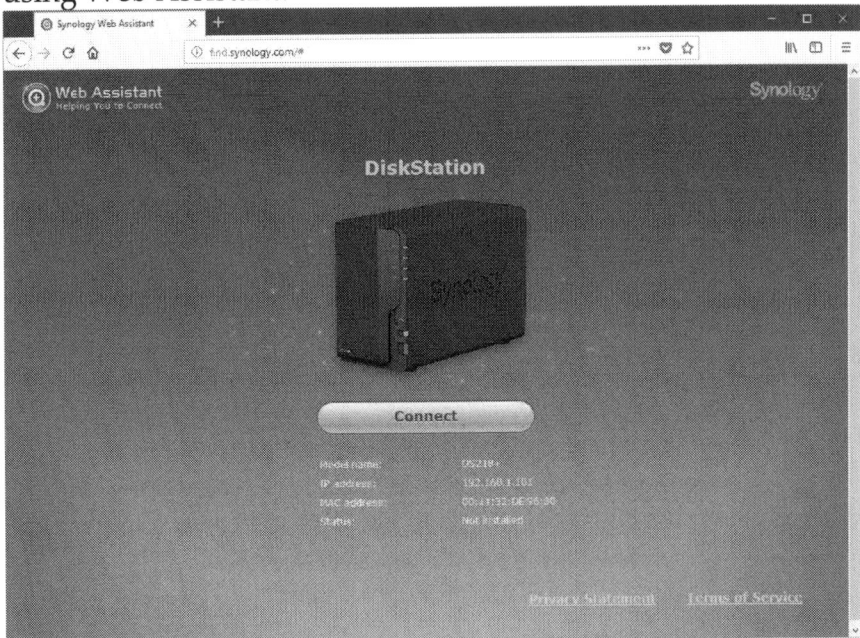

Figure 2: Web Assistant – click Connect

Click **Connect.** Acknowledge the Synology End User License Agreement. On the next screen click the **Set up** button and the following screen is shown. You would normally click the **Install Now** button, which will automatically download and install the latest version of the DSM firmware. However, there are also options to download a different version from the Synology website, or to browse the computer and install a copy that has downloaded previously:

—

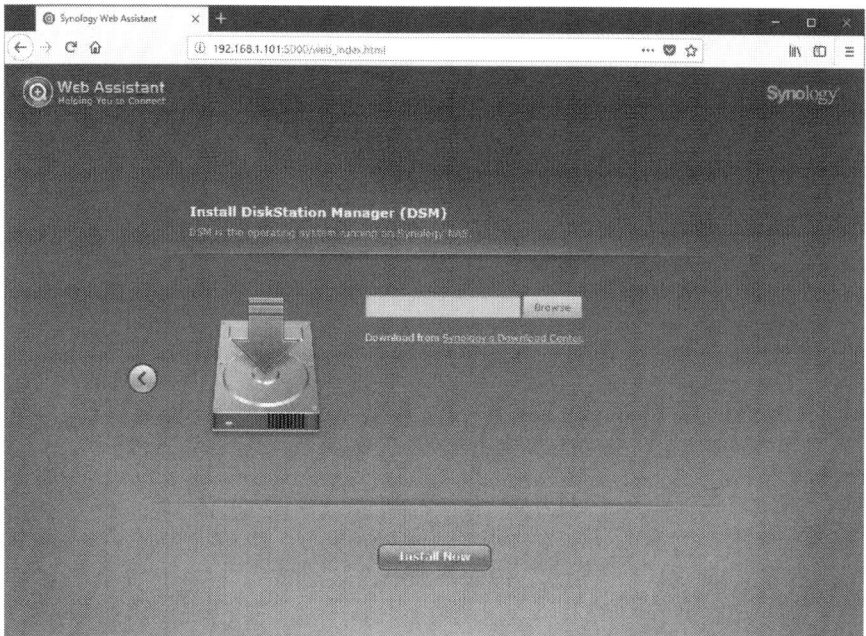

Figure 3: Web Assistant –click Install Now

A warning message is displayed, stating that any data on the hard drive(s) will be destroyed. Acknowledge this warning and click **OK**. The installation will now proceed, during which time a status screen is displayed. Do not click the screen or close the browser whilst the installation is running. After installation is completed – which typically takes around 10 minutes – the following screen is displayed. Give the server a name – it is suggested that you simply call it *server*, although if you have or envisage having further DiskStations you may want to use a logical naming scheme e.g. *server1, server2* and so on. For the *Username*, specify *admin*. Enter and confirm a password: use something non-obvious and preferably a mixture of upper and lower case letters, numbers and symbols and which does not include the username. DSM will provide feedback on the strength of the password: you want something that it considers to be 'strong'. Click **Next**:

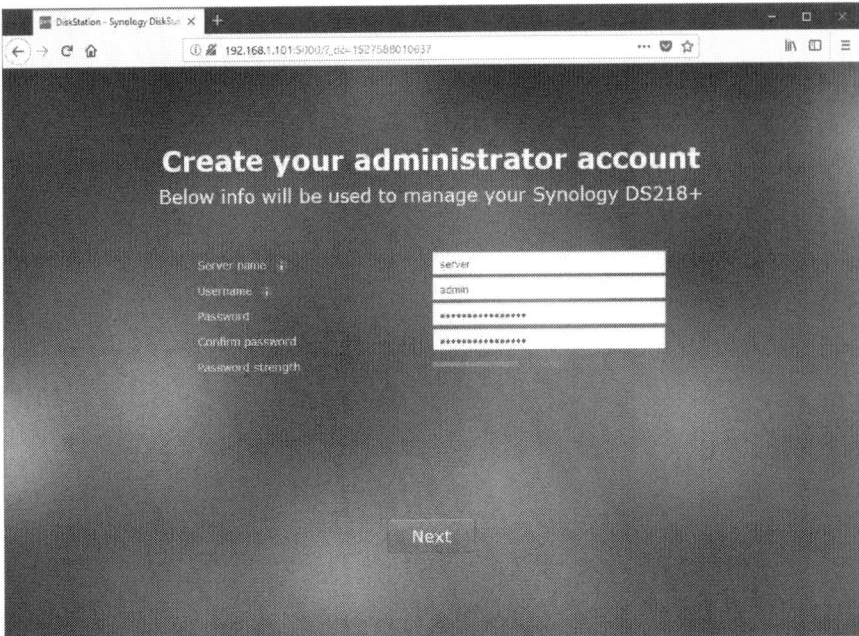

Figure 4: Create administrator account

A screen that simply reads 'Congratulations' shortly appears – click **Next**. On the subsequent screen you specify the *DSM Update & Maintenance* settings. You cannot progress unless you choose an update option; it is suggested you choose **Install the important updates of DSM automatically** and accept the default settings (the settings can always be changed later – why and how to is discussed in section **9.7 Checking for DSM Updates**). Click **Next**:

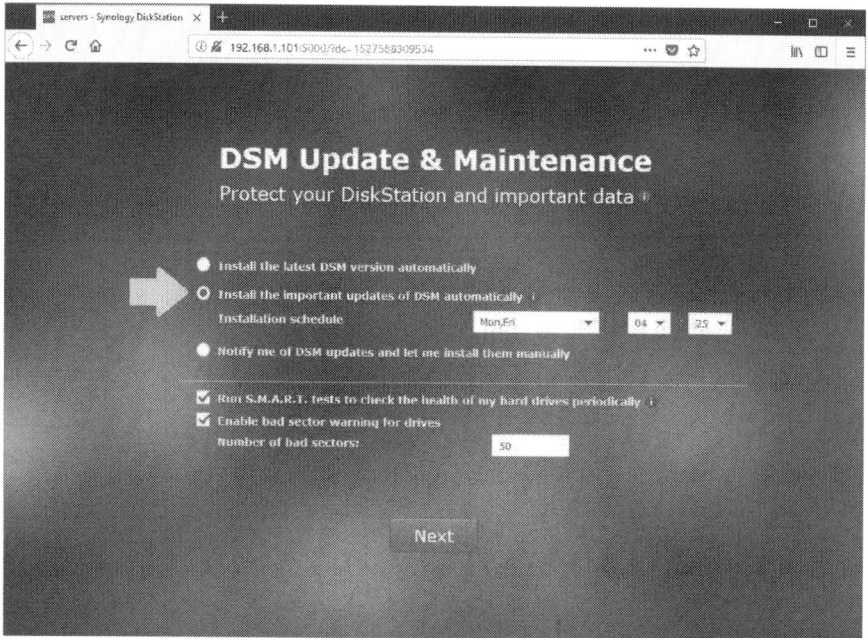

Figure 5: DSM Update Settings

The next screen is for setting up *QuickConnect*, which is Synology's easy method for providing remote access to the DiskStation. However, it is suggested that you defer this step for now - we will return to it in section **2.7 QuickConnect: The Key to Remote Connectivity** - which you can do by clicking the **Skip this step** link at the bottom of the screen. There will be a warning message about the implications of this, but just click **Yes** to continue:

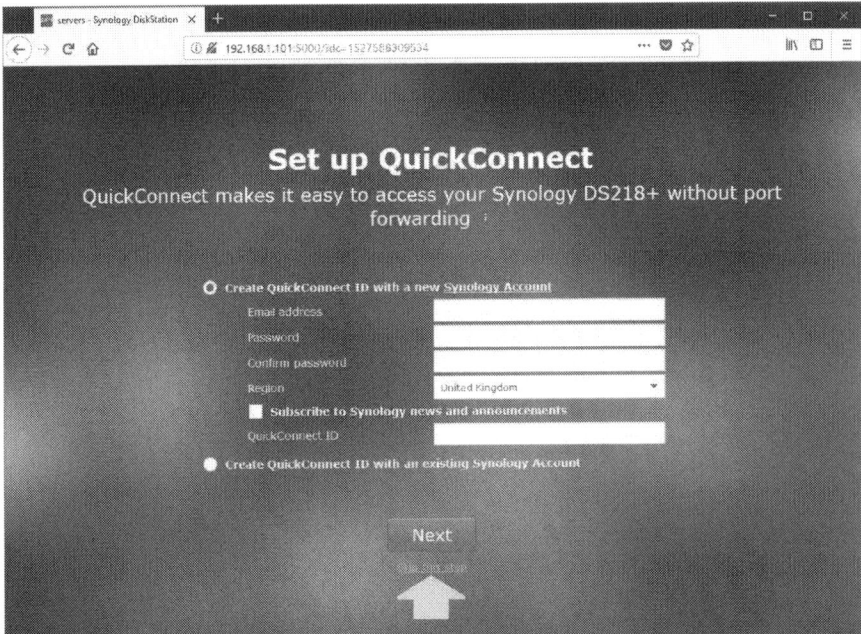

Figure 6: QuickConnect screen (skip for now)

The subsequent screen offers a selection of recommended packages – apps that provide additional functionality and which transform the DiskStation from being just a storage device into something that can do a lot more. If you are a home user you may wish to click **Install**; if you are a 'strictly business' user then you may want to click **Skip this step** as many of the apps are concerned with multimedia, which may not be a requirement (either way, how to add or remove packages will be covered later on in the guide). If you opt to install the packages, you will need to accept Terms of Service and Privacy statements. Click **OK**.

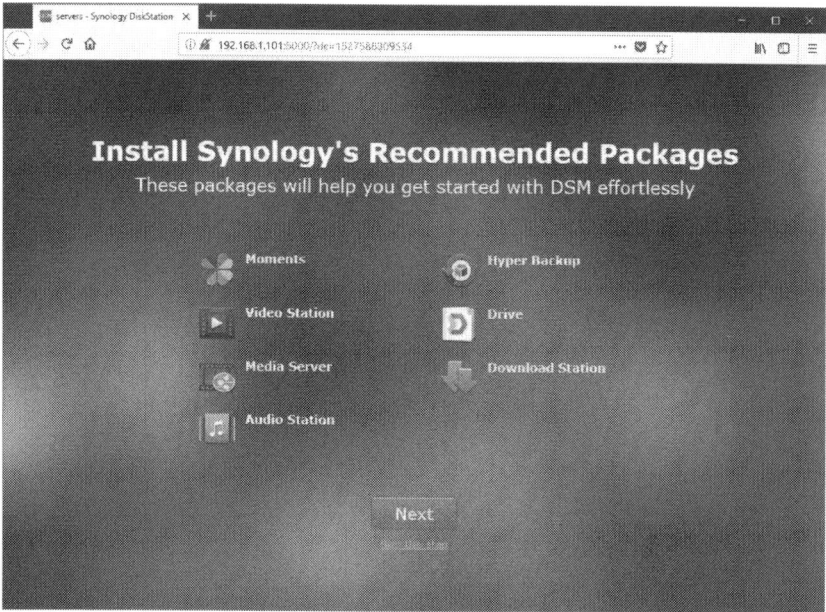

Figure 7: Install Recommended Packages screen

When everything is ready, the following screen will be shown. It is not necessary to tick the box about sharing network location information with Synology, you can just click **Go**:

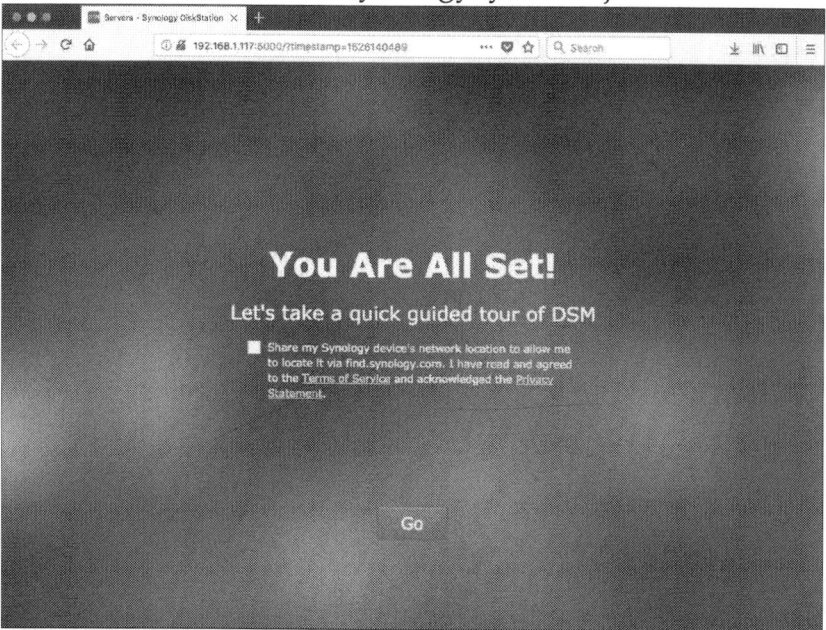

Figure 8: Completion screen

2.2 Five Minute Tour of DiskStation Manager

After clicking **Go,** the main Desktop is shown (although you may receive a notice about 'Device Analytics', which you need to accept). The first time you login to DSM, a selection of tips is presented – just click anywhere on the screen to work through them. Then, the DSM Help system is displayed; this covers a number of topics and can be read through if required or at a later date (or not at all – everything useful you need to know is in this book!). Tick the box so it does not automatically launch every time you login, click **OK** and then close the help screen by clicking the cross (X) in the top right-hand corner.

Having closed the help panel, you will be presented with the main DSM screen, which will look straightforward to anyone who has used a Windows PC or Mac. There is a Desktop area, which can be customized. There are a number of icons on the Desktop. There is something akin to a menu bar and taskbar at the top of the screen:

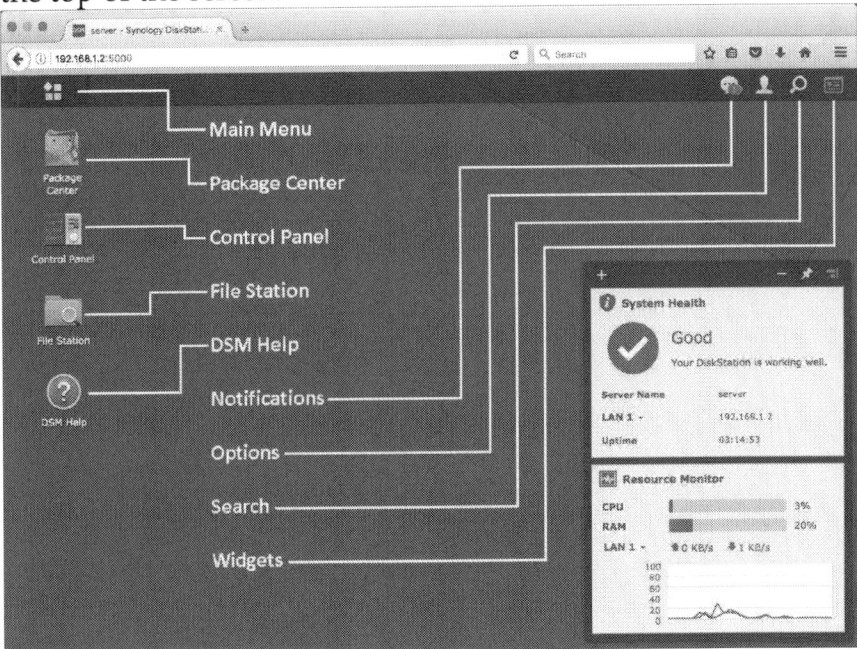

Figure 9: Overview of Desktop

26

The *Main Menu* provides access to important system programs. When clicked it expands, displaying icons which are then clicked to run the underlying programs. The icons can also be dragged onto the Desktop for convenience and this has already been done for a number of them (*Control Panel, File Station, Package Center* and *DSM Help*). When a program is running, its icon appears on the taskbar and you can right-click to fix it there permanently. To close the Main Menu, click anywhere within it or click its icon in the top left-hand corner of the screen. Note that if you chose or allowed the installation of additional packages during setup, you may have some additional icons to those shown below:

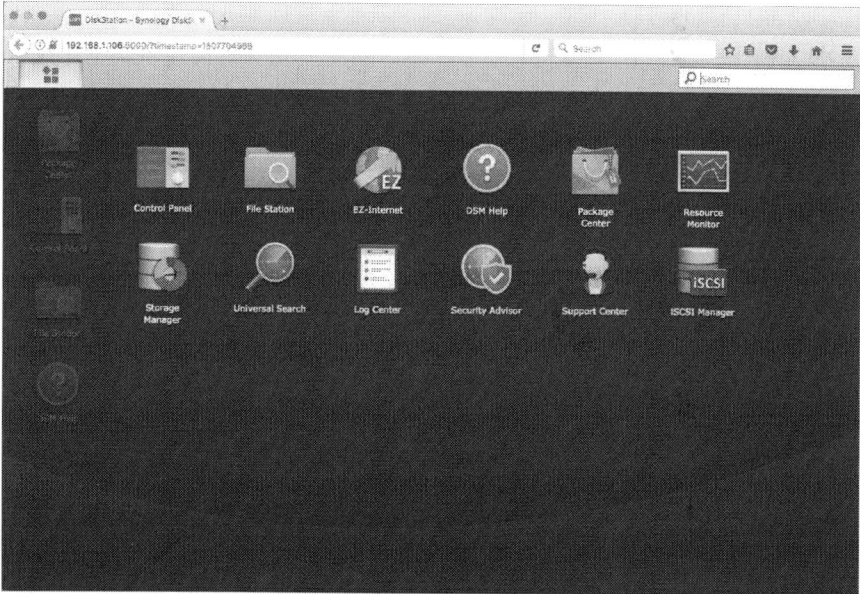

Figure 10: The Main Menu

The *Control Panel* provides icons to setup and customize the DiskStation, grouped into four main categories (*File Sharing, Connectivity, System* and *Applications*) and again, icons can be dragged onto the Desktop for convenience.

The Control Panel has two views or *modes*, controlled by a toggle in the top right-hand corner: *Basic Mode*, which shows a subset of the available icons grouped (and one less category) and *Advanced Mode*, which shows all of them. Throughout this guide we will assume that you are viewing the Control Panel in Advanced mode. The term 'Advanced' is a misnomer, so do not let the terminology discourage you:

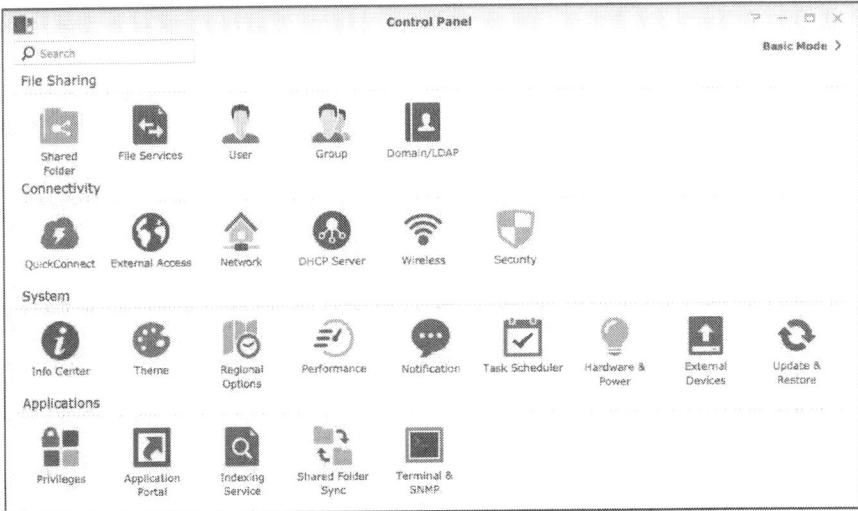

Figure 11: The Control Panel

File Station displays the contents of the disk volumes and folders and can be used for manipulating files, similar in principle to Windows Explorer/File Explorer on a PC or the Finder on a Mac. The first time you launch it there may be a message to advise that no shared folders currently exist and it will assist you in creating one – you can defer it for now by clicking **Cancel** as we will return to it shortly.

The *Package Center* is used for downloading and maintaining applications from Synology that provide additional capabilities, such as security and multimedia – you may recall that we skipped this topic during the installation process, but it will be returned to later in **9.1 Package Center**.

The *DSM Help* icon does what the name suggests. The help system operates in two modes: if the DiskStation is connected to the internet then the help is 'live' from Synology, meaning it is always up-to-date. However, if the DiskStation is not connected to the internet, then it falls back to a more limited version already built-in to DSM. The help system is searchable and also includes tutorials, frequently asked questions and video tutorials.

Notifications provide status information about events that have occurred e.g. backup successfully completed or any system errors.

Widgets are small panels that provide status information, many of which relate to the health of the system. These can also be dragged onto the Desktop to further customize it and by default some widgets for monitoring system status are already present in the bottom right-hand corner of the screen. Widgets can be pinned, removed, moved about and so on.

Search, as the name suggests, enables you to search files and file contents. The first time it is run, you will need to click to create the indexing.

The *Options* icon provides some configuration choices and is used for logging out, restarting and shutting down the system. Note that NAS devices are commonly left running 24x7 and only the admin user can shutdown the system.

2.3 Configure Networking

The first thing we need to do is make a decision about the IP address for the DiskStation. Every device has a number within a network to uniquely identify it, known as the *IP address*. The router itself will have a default fixed IP address decided by the manufacturer, for instance 192.168.1.1 or 192.168.1.254 is a common choice. It will then allocate numbers to computers and devices as they connect, for example the first computer might become 192.168.1.101, the second computer might become 192.168.1.102 and so on. A piece of software inside the router – known as a *DHCP server* – handles this process. The 'D' in DHCP stands for dynamic and indicates that the IP addresses are handled dynamically and recycled. So, for example, the next time the first computer is switched on it might be allocated a different number, say 192.168.1.108. The fact that the numbers change does not make any difference to computers but some devices prefer a fixed address, which is why routers have them.

During the installation the DiskStation received an IP address from the router's DHCP server. However, servers and NAS boxes work better with fixed addresses so we need to change matters. Click **Control Panel** followed by **Network** and the **Network Interface** tab. There will be several entries, typically *LAN*, *PPPoE* and *IPv6 Tunneling*. If the DiskStation has multiple network adapters then there will be *LAN 1, LAN 2* etc. The first or only *LAN* entry will have a status of 'Connected' – click to highlight it then click the **Edit** button:

—

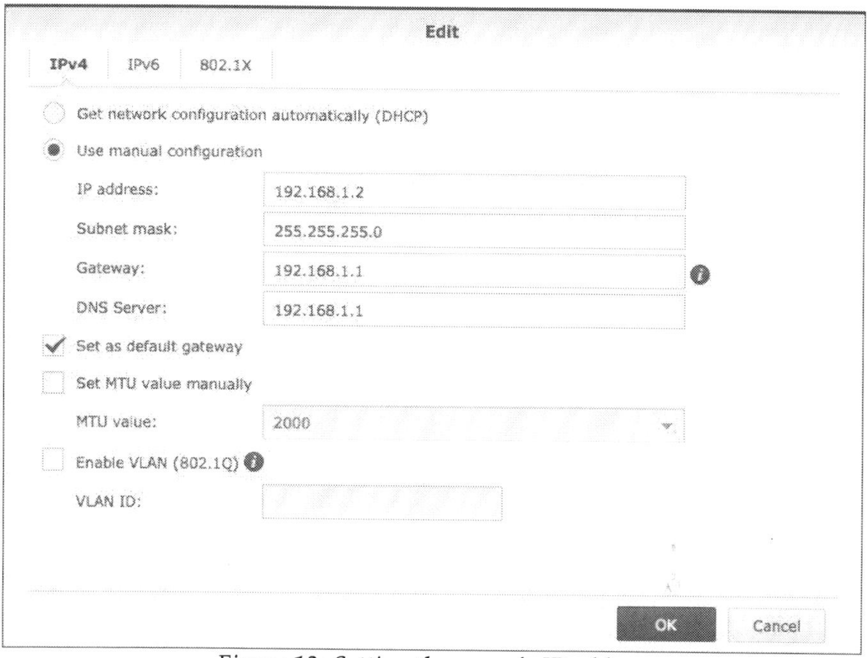

Figure 12: Setting the server's IP address

On the *IPv4* tab, click **Use manual configuration** and specify an IP address that is close to that of the router, which is shown on the screen under the alternative name of *Gateway*. In this example, the router/Gateway is 192.168.1.1, so a suitable address would be something like 192.168.1.2. The *Subnet mask* should be set to 255.255.255.0, then click **OK**. Note that having made a change to the IP address, you may lose connectivity to the DiskStation and have to refresh the browser.

2.4 Power Management

DiskStations have various options relating to power management, some of which are concerned with energy saving and can be used to reduce power consumption and potentially save money. To configure, go into **Control Panel** and click **Hardware & Power** to display the following panel. The options available vary depending on the model of the DiskStation, so there can be some variations in this screen:

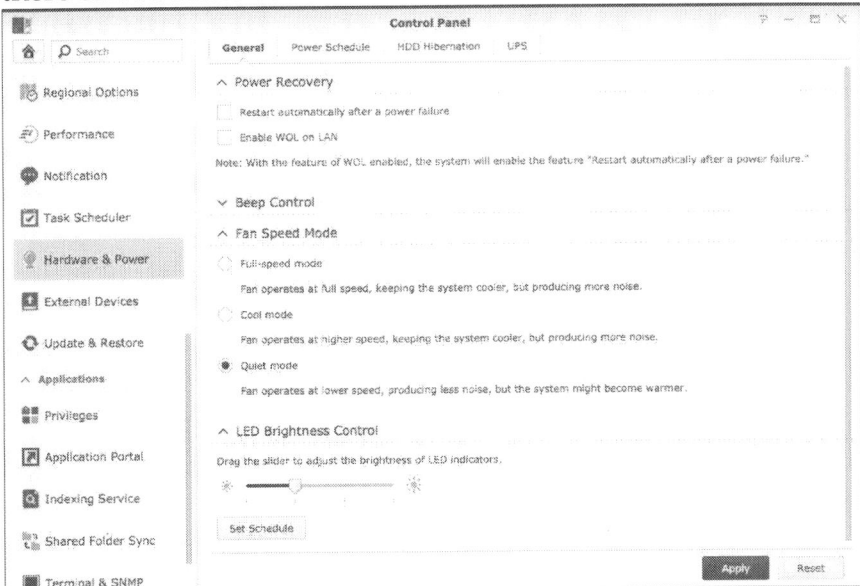

Figure 13: Control Panel for Hardware & Power

On the **General** tab, tick **Restart automatically after a power failure**. In the event that electrical power is ever disrupted, this will cause the server to restart itself upon resumption of power. The *Beep Control* section defines the error conditions which will cause the DiskStation to make a beeping noise.

Set the *Fan Speed Mode* to **Quiet Mode** if the DiskStation is located in a quiet area (e.g. at home) or to **Cool Mode** is a small amount of noise is acceptable (e.g. typical office environment). If the DiskStation is located in a warm place, or where noise is unimportant, you may want to set it to **Full-speed Mode**.

On some DiskStations, it is possible to set the brightness of the LED indicators on the unit, using the slider in the LED Brightness Control section. This can reduce power consumption, or reduce distraction if the DiskStation is located in a bedroom or next to a television set. It is also possible to set a schedule so this happens at particular times e.g. overnight, by clicking the **Set Schedule** button then clicking in the resultant matrix:

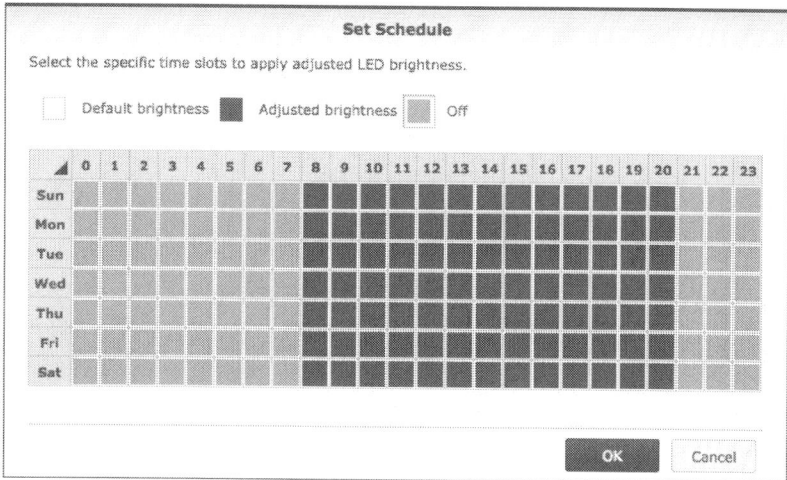

Figure 14: Setting the schedule for LED brightness

In a similar manner, if there is a **Power Schedule** tab – which there is on most models – the DiskStation can be scheduled to power itself on and off automatically. Doing this can save on energy costs and enhance security. However, note that if this is done then it is important to ensure that the DiskStation will not be powered down when an activity such as backup or an anti-virus scan is scheduled to take place.

To create a schedule, click the **Create** button on the **Power Schedule** tab. Specify whether the event is to Startup or Shutdown the server and whether it is to run daily, weekly or at weekends (it is also possible to specify particular days of the week). Then click on **OK** followed by the **Save** button. Make sure the task is **Enabled**, which it should be if it has just been created:

—

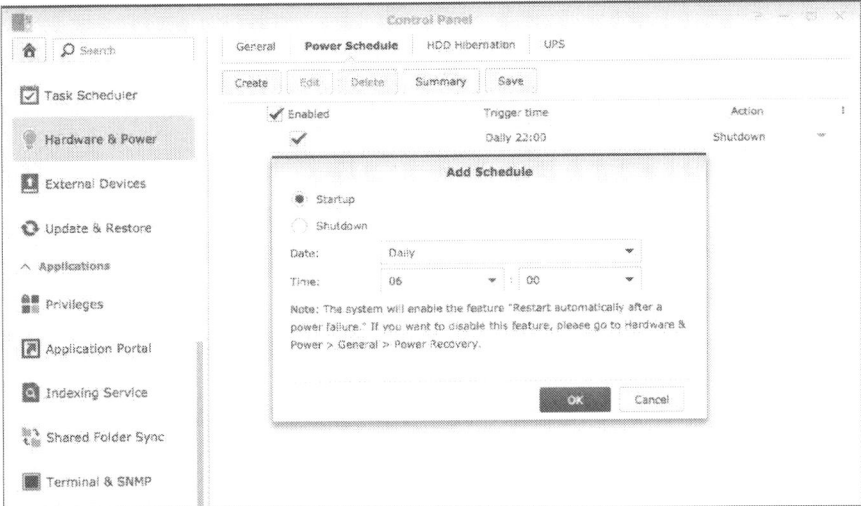

Figure 15: Power – adding a schedule

Using the **HDD Hibernation** tab, the hard disk(s) can be programmed to hibernate after a set period. This also saves energy, but may result in a short delay when someone attempts to access the DiskStation, typically in the order of about 15-30 seconds, whilst the disks spin up. The default hibernation time of 20 minutes is suitable in most cases; any external USB hard drives (e.g. backup drives) can also be made to hibernate. Again, note that there may be some minor variations in this screen depending on the model:

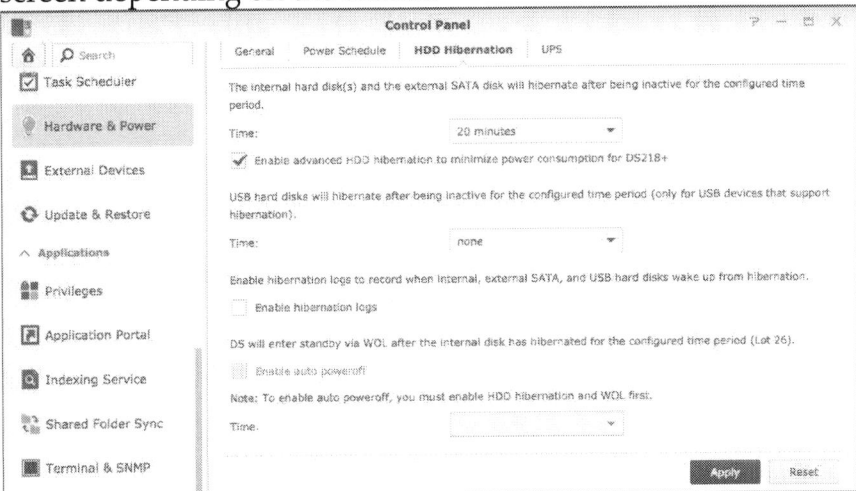

Figure 16: Hard Disk Hibernation settings

2.5 File Services

File Services refers to the means by which DSM provides access to files and folders for different types of client computers. These clients can be Windows PCs, Macs, or Linux machines. Other devices (e.g. tablets and smartphones) may be able to access files on the DiskStation if they understand the underlying protocols associated with these computer types.

By default, the Synology installation assumes that you will be using Windows PCs and Macs and it is not generally necessary to change any of the settings for File Services. So, most people reading this can simply skip to the next section now. However, if any of the following conditions are true, then you may need to make changes:

- The Windows workgroup is not called *Workgroup* (although it usually is)
- You want to backup Macs to the server using Time Machine
- You need to make a shared printer available to Mac clients
- You wish to use Linux or other Unix-based computers in an advanced manner

Windows Computers

To change settings, go to the **Control Panel,** click the **File Services** icon and in it click the **SMB/AFP/NFS** tab. If your workgroup is not called *Workgroup,* in the *SMB* section change the name of the **Workgroup** to match that of your computers. Note: having to do this would be unusual as *WORKGROUP* is the default name on Windows computers. There are also some options and advanced settings relating to the SMB protocol and which may be of interest to experienced Windows Server administrators.

Macs

Historically, Apple computers used a network protocol called AFP (*Apple Filing Protocol*) whilst Windows computers used SMB (Server Message Block). However, beginning with OS X 10.9 ('Mavericks') Macs switched to SMB for their default network protocol, too. In theory, you could operate without AFP, but it is recommended that you keep the AFP service enabled. You will certainly need it if you are using older versions of OS X.

If you are planning to use Time Machine – which is covered in detail in section **7.6 Backing Up Macs using Time Machine** – click the **Advanced** tab within **File Services**. Make sure all the boxes in the Bonjour section are ticked, then click **Apply**. You will receive a warning message that SMB3 will also be enabled – this is fine, so click **Yes**.

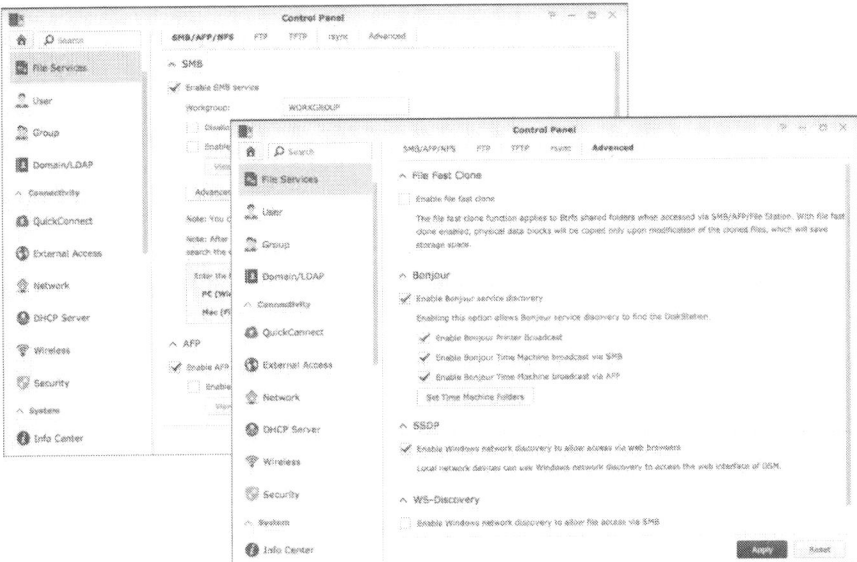

Figure 17: File Services

Linux Computers

Most Linux distributions include the ability to connect to SMB-supporting systems, such as DSM. Unless you have a specific need, you may find it easier to use SMB, in which case you do not need to do anything additional. However, if you use Linux or other Unix-type variant computers in an 'advanced' manner – defined here as specific use of the NFS protocol – you will need to enable NFS on the DiskStation. Within **Control Panel,** click the **File Services** icon and on it click the **SMB/AFP/NFS** tab. Under the **NFS File Service** section, click the **Enable NFS** tick-box. There are also some options and advanced settings, which may be of interest to experienced Linux/Unix users.

A range of other tabs enable other file services to be setup, although some of these are more specialized and may be of little interest to typical home and small business users.

2.6 Overview of Storage in DSM

Storage management is quite sophisticated in DSM, as it is designed to cater for a wide variety of scenarios, ranging from home users with a single DiskStation with one hard drive, through to mission-critical enterprise setups with hundreds of DiskStations, thousands of drives and Petabytes of data. Here's the bottom line: when you install DSM using Web Assistant, then everything is taken care of for you, with the system making the right decisions on your behalf. For instance, if your DiskStation has two hard drives it will be configured for SHR (Synology Hybrid RAID, as described in section **1.3 RAID**). If your DiskStation has a sufficiently powerful processor, it will format the drives using an advanced filing system called *Btrfs* (sometimes pronounced 'Butter-F-S'), otherwise the drives are formatted using the *ext4* filing system. It is possible to change matters using a tool called *Storage Manager* located on the Main Menu, but this is quite an advanced topic and outside the scope of this guide. For the most part, everything 'just works' and if you are happy with that you can skip to the next section. The following notes are by way of background for those who are interested in such things.

The basic principle is that a DiskStation contains a number of drives, which can be conventional mechanical drives (HDD) or solid state drives (SSD). These drives are consolidated to create one or more *Storage Pools*, which can be optimized for better performance or flexibility. One or more volumes are created on the storage pool(s), and these volumes are then usually configured with a RAID scheme. The available RAID schemes depend on the number of drives, but Synology recommends SHR for most users.

The volumes themselves are formatted using the Btrfs or ext4 filing systems: ext4 is from the Linux world and will work on all DiskStations; Btrfs supports advanced features including shared folder snapshots and replication, advanced data integrity and containers. If you ever receive a choice between Btrfs and ext4 when using the DiskStation, go for the former.

Setting up storage and the use of features such as Snapshots and iSCSI are covered in the CTACS *Synology NAS Setup Guide for Home & Small Business*.

2.7 QuickConnect: The Key to Remote Connectivity

Remote access has two aspects. Firstly, there are the actual capabilities: cloud storage, syncing, backup and so on that DSM and the optional packages provide. The second aspect is how to connect the DiskStation to the internet and be able to access it in a simple, secure and safe manner. This is what *QuickConnect* does: it provides an easy, straightforward mechanism for remote access, suitable for most home and small business users. It works as a relay service, passing data to and from computers and the DiskStation over the internet via Synology. No data is stored at Synology itself and it remains *your* data on *your* computers. Because the service uses standard web protocols, it avoids the need for techniques such as port forwarding, router configuration and domain services. This also means remote access can be made available in many places where there may be no option to make technical changes to the underlying environment, such as in schools, colleges, corporate workplaces and so on.

Launch **QuickConnect** by clicking on the icon in the **Control Panel**. To use the service, you need an account with Synology, which you can obtain instantly and freely by clicking **Log in to or register a Synology Account**. Note: if you already have a Synology account and a QuickConnect ID (for instance, this is not your first Synology) you can re-use them rather than have to register for new ones.

Having registered, tick the **Enable QuickConnect** box and enter a *QuickConnect ID* of your choosing. The QuickConnect ID must begin with a letter and can contain a mixture of letters, numbers and dashes e.g. *acme1234*. Click **Apply**. Assuming all is well, after a few seconds the QuickConnect screen will update and give you an external internet address - known as the *hostname* - for the DiskStation.

This takes the form of *http://QuickConnect.to/nnnnnn*
e.g. *http://QuickConnect.to/acme1234*.

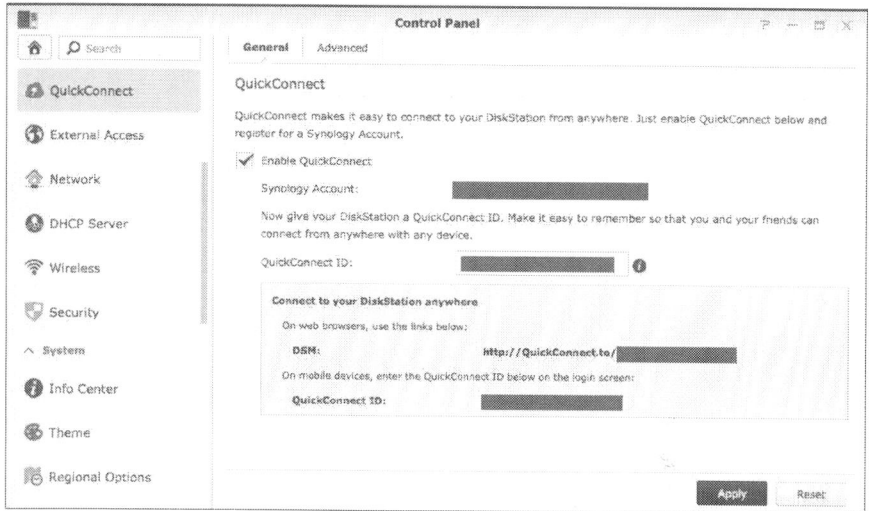

Figure 18: Setting up QuickConnect

Assuming no problems, you can now test the system. Go to a computer, launch the browser (e.g. Internet Explorer, Firefox) and enter the hostname that you were assigned e.g. *http://QuickConnect.to/acme1234* or whatever it is. After a few seconds, you should be greeted with the standard DSM logon screen.

3 SHARED FOLDERS

The main purpose of most networks is to provide an environment for users to safely store and share information. This is done by creating folders on the server, some shared and some private, then defining access rights to control who sees what. The structure of these folders will depend upon the requirements of the household or organization, but a typical starting arrangement might be:

- A shared folder that everyone has access to
- Individual private home folders for each user
- Folders for music, photos and videos (particularly so for a home system)
- A location to store master copies of programs, drivers, utilities and so on

3.1 Creating a Shared Folder

To create a shared folder, go to **Control Panel > Shared Folder** and click **Create**, which will cause the *Shared Folder Creation Wizard* to run. Our first folder will be a shared folder for everyone to use and to make this very obvious, we will give it a name of *shared*; you can optionally specify a *Description*. If you have multiple volumes on the system, you can make use of the *Location* drop-down to define where it will be. Tick the **Hide sub-folders and files from users without permissions** box. If you want to be able to recover files that have been deleted tick the **Enable Recycle Bin** and **Restrict access to administrators only** boxes. Then click **OK**:

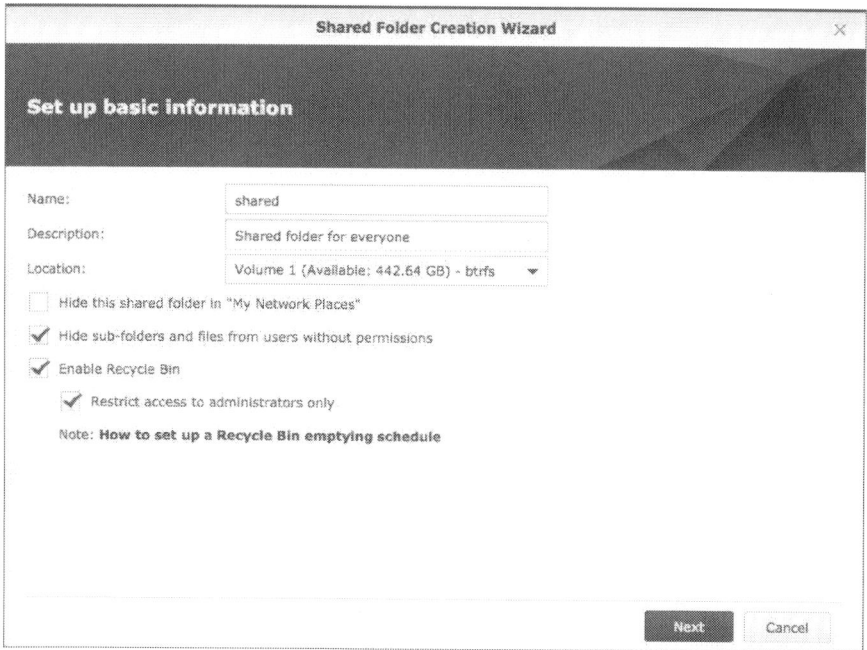

Figure 19: Creating a shared folder

On the next screen, there is the option to encrypt the folder. This provides a higher level of security by encrypting the contents of the folder; in the event that the hard disks were removed from the DiskStation and loaded onto another computer system, it would not be possible to read the contents of the folder unless the other party had a copy of the encryption key. If you are storing confidential information you may wish to encrypt the folders, but be aware that there is no way to recover the data if the encryption key is lost plus an additional feature called *Key Manager* needs to be enabled. Because of these considerations, only encrypt folders when you need to do so and not as a matter of course. To create an encrypted folder, tick the **Encrypt this shared folder** box and enter and confirm the encryption key; the key needs to be at least 8 characters in length and you should use something obscure, such as a mixture of random letters and numerals. Click **Next**.

A panel to *Configure advanced settings* is then shown. If the folder is being created on a volume that has been formatted with Btrfs, then options to check data integrity and set a folder quota (size) become available, although there may be some performance implications. If the volume is ext4, these options are not available. Click **Next**. A *Confirm settings* screen is displayed – click **Apply** to create the folder.

Having created the folder, you will be taken into a screen that defines permissions for the users, meaning who has access to the folder and what type of access. There are three basic types of access: *Read/Write* (do anything); *Read only* (access it, but no changes allowed); *No access*, along with a *Custom* option. This is a chicken-and-egg situation, as we have yet to create any users (covered in section **4.2 Creating a User**). For now, give *admin* **Read/Write** access, give *guest* **No access** and click **OK**. If you need to return to this screen on a subsequent occasion, go into **Shared Folder**, highlight the folder, click **Edit** then click the **Permissions** tab.

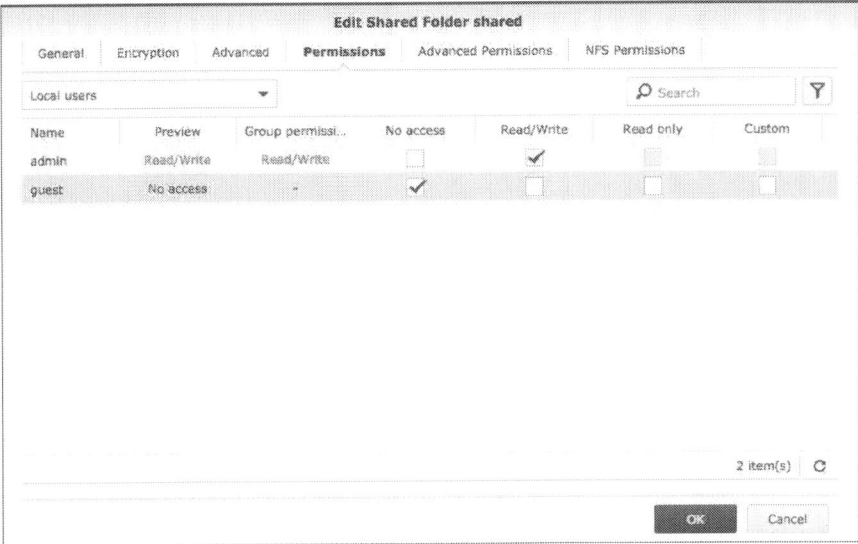

Edit Shared Folder shared						
General	Encryption	Advanced	**Permissions**	Advanced Permissions	NFS Permissions	
Local users ▼					Search	▼
Name	Preview	Group permissi...	No access	Read/Write	Read only	Custom
admin	Read/Write	Read/Write	☐	✓	☐	☐
guest	No access	-	✓	☐	☐	☐
					2 item(s)	⟳
					OK	Cancel

Figure 20: Shared folder permissions

Now repeat the entire process and create folders called *music*, *photo* and *video* in the same manner. Optionally, create a further folder called *technical*, this time with the **Hide this shared folder in My Network Places** box ticked in addition to the **Hide folders and files from users without permissions** box.

3.2 Enabling Home Folders

The folders that have just been created are shared folders, potentially for the use of everyone on the network. It is also a good idea to create *home folders*, one for each user, where they can store things that only that individual needs access to, analogous to the Documents folder on their personal computers. To enable home folders, click **Control Panel,** then **User** followed by the **Advanced** tab. In the *User Home* section, which is towards the bottom of the screen, tick the **Enable user home service** box. If you have multiple volumes in the system (not generally the case on a small setup) you can optionally specify a *Location*. If you want users to be able to recover their deleted items, tick **Enable Recycle Bin**. Click **Apply**. This will result in home folders being created automatically for any users that are subsequently defined.

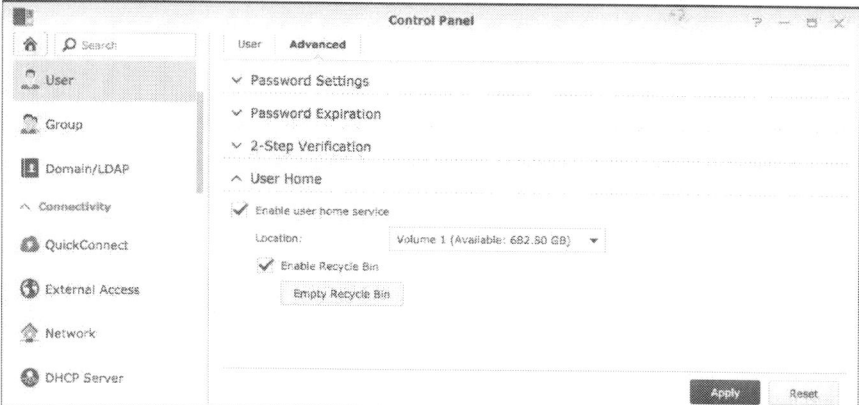

Figure 21: Enable user home service

Having enabled the User home service, go back to **Control Panel** and click on **Shared Folder**. Highlight the entry for the *homes* folder and click **Edit**. Tick the **Hide this shared folder in 'My Network Places'** and **Hide sub-folders and files from users without permissions** boxes and click **OK**. The Control Panel should now appear along the following lines:

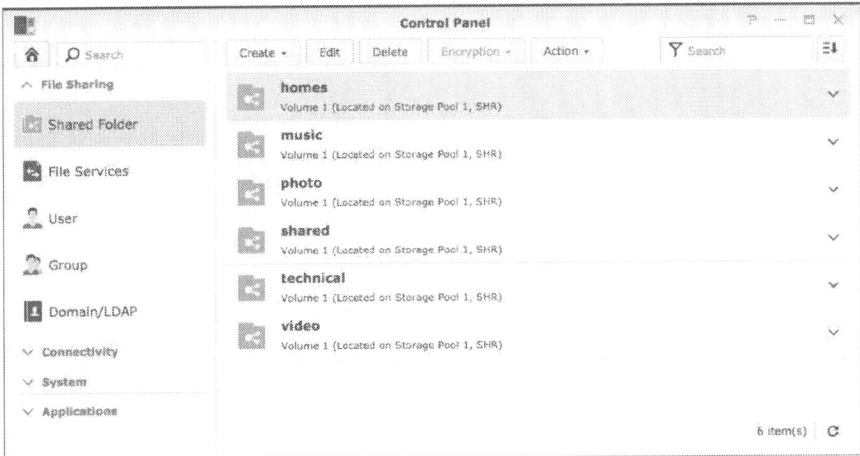

Figure 22: List of shared folders

It will now be possible to view the folders from computers on the network:

Windows: Choose **Start > Run** and type in *server* (you will probably be prompted to enter the admin id and password for the DiskStation). Note that to view the hidden technical folder it is necessary to type *server\technical*. If this does not work, type in the IP address of the server instead e.g. *192.168.1.2\technical* in our example.

Mac: Go into Finder and in the *Shared* section highlight the entry for *server*. Click **Connect As...** and enter the admin id and password of the DiskStation.

3.3 Deleting or Changing a Shared Folder

Should it ever be necessary to change a shared folder, for instance, to rename or delete it, this has to be done from the **Shared Folder** option in **Control Panel** (specifically, it cannot be done from *File Station* - this is a common error which catches some people out). Highlight the folder and click the **Delete** button; there will be a warning message that has to be acknowledged, plus it is then necessary to enter the admin password as an additional safety check.

4 USERS

To access the DiskStation, it is necessary to have a *user account* on it. During the installation of DSM an initial user was created – *admin*. If you are the only person who will ever use the DiskStation, you can work with that user account for everything and skip this chapter altogether. However, if other people will also be using the DiskStation, such as in a home, business or educational environment, then you will need to create user accounts for them.

4.1 Naming Conventions

This is one area where a different approach can be taken depending on whether it is a home or business network. In the case of a home network the user names can be just about anything you want, although there is some sense in following a scheme. For instance, you could use the first names of the family or household members.

In a business environment a more formal approach is often appropriate. As a general point, the greater consistency there is then the better things will be. For user names, two common conventions are to use the first name plus the initial of the surname, or the initial of the first name plus the surname, although in some parts of the world other conventions might be more appropriate. In the case of particularly long names and double barreled names, it might be an idea to abbreviate them.

For example:

Name of Person	User Name	or	User Name
Nick Rushton	nickr		nrushton
Mary O'Hara	maryoh		mohara
Ian Smith	ians		ismith
Amber Williams	amberw		awilliams
Daniela Petrova	danielap		dpetrova

4.2 Creating a User

To create a user, go to **Control Panel** and click the **User** icon. On the **User** tab click the **Create** button. The *Create* button is actually a drop-down with three entries: the first is to create a single user and the one we will use; the second is to import a list of names to be turned into users which is useful in, say, a larger organization; the third is to copy a user. As a household or small business will typically have a relatively small number of users we will create them one at a time. Enter: the user's login name; an optional description for them e.g. their full name; a password and its confirmation. The best passwords are non-obvious and comprise a mixture of upper and lower case letters, mixed with numbers and symbols; DSM can also generate a random password if preferred. By default, DSM requires a password of at least six characters (to control this behaviour see section **9.4 Password Settings**). Optionally, click the **Disallow the user to change account password** box (this can be useful in schools with young children). It is not necessary to specify the email address or send a notification to the newly created user. Click **Next**.

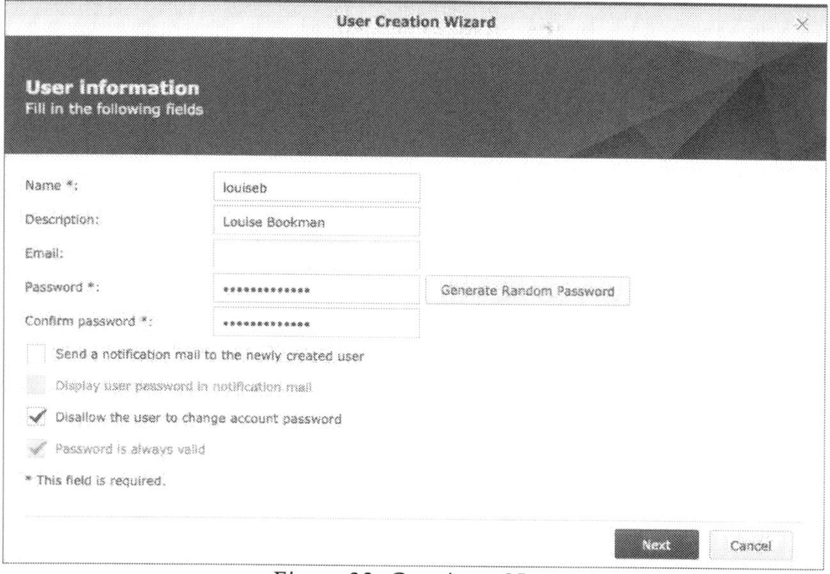

Figure 23: Creating a User

On the subsequent screen check that they are a member of the *users* group. Do not make them a member of the administrators group as access so this should be restricted. Click **Next**:

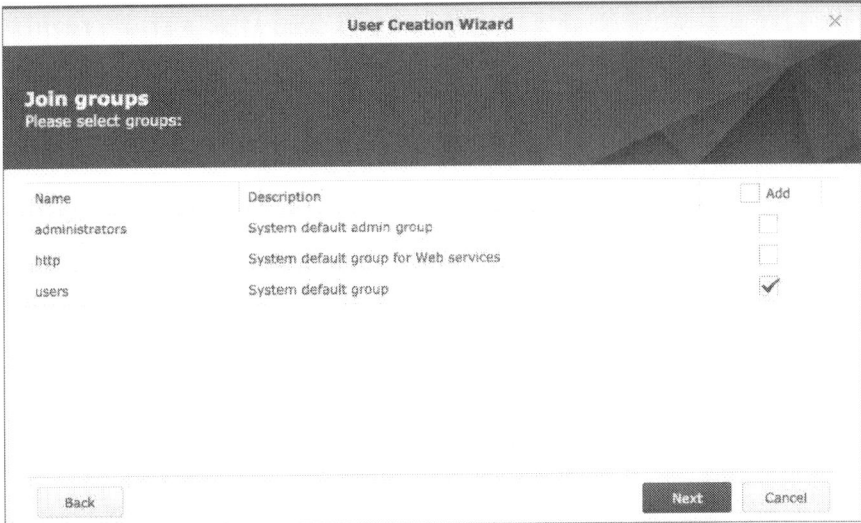

Figure 24: Joining a Group

The following screen defines which folders the user has access to. The three choices are: *Read only*, meaning that the user can use the files in the folder but cannot update them or add to the folder; *Read/Write*, meaning they can do anything with the folder; *No access*, meaning they have no access at all to the folder. Set the appropriate permissions as follows: **Read/Write** to *music, photo, shared* and *video*; **No access** to *technical*; leave *homes* blank. Click **Next**.

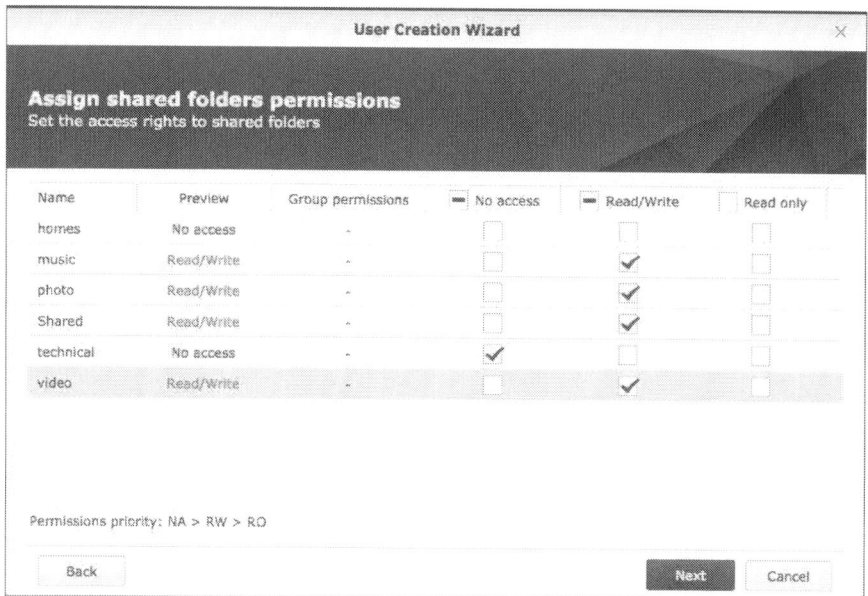

Figure 25: Assigning shared folder permissions

The follow-on screen is for setting a storage quota i.e. how much disk space in Gigabytes (GB) or Megabytes (MB) the user is permitted. As disk space is cheap and plentiful this is not commonly done in a home or small business setting, so ignore this step by clicking **Next**. The subsequent screen controls which applications the user can access. Generally speaking, everyone should have access to *File Station* and *DSM* but the other applications would only be if specifically needed. Click **Next**. Note that if applications are subsequently installed from the *Package Center* then this list of applications may gain additional entries and it may be necessary to revisit the users' settings:

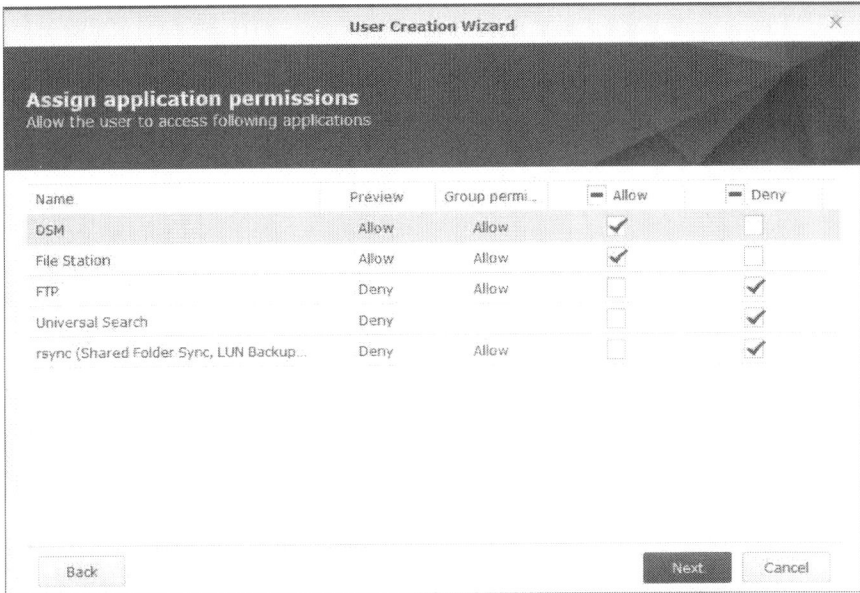

Figure 26: Assigning application permissions

The following screen is for controlling the speed of access to certain applications. Again, this is not something that would usually be bothered with, so just click **Next** to ignore it. Finally, a *Confirm Settings* screen is displayed - click **Apply** to proceed and the user will be created within a few seconds, with their details then listed on the main User panel.

This process should be repeated until all the users have been created. If you have many users to create, you may find it helpful to first create a checklist of their names and to make a note of the passwords.

4.3 Modifying, Deleting and Copying Users

To modify a user, go to **Control Panel > User**. Click the user's name to highlight it then click the **Edit** button. This provides access to the information that was specified when the user was created and which can now be modified. For instance, the user's password can be changed on the **Info** panel. Having made any changes click **OK**.

To delete a user, go to **Control Panel > User**. Click on the user's name to highlight it then click the **Delete** button. A warning message is displayed, advising that the user's data will be deleted. Acknowledge it and click **Delete**.

To create a new user more quickly by copying an existing one, go to **Control Panel > User**. Highlight an existing user, click the **Create** dropdown and choose **Copy user**. This will invoke the first panel of the *User Creation Wizard*; it is only necessary to enter the new user's name, password and password confirmation, click **Next** and then **Apply** on the Confirm settings screen. The new user will have exactly the same permissions and characteristics as the original user.

5 ACCESSING THE DISKSTATION

There are multiple methods for accessing the DiskStation; some of these are specific to Windows only, some to Mac only, whereas some work for most platforms. There are also apps available for smartphones and tablets.

5.1 Using a Browser

This is the universal method for accessing the DiskStation and works for Windows PCs, Macs, Linux computers and Chromebooks. Simply go to any computer on the local network, launch a browser such as Firefox, Internet Explorer, Chrome or Safari and type in the name or IP address of the server e.g. *server, 192.168.1.2* etc. The standard DSM login screen is displayed; the user should enter their name and password and they will be presented with a fairly minimalist Desktop; in essence, all they can access is File Station (unless additional options have been granted to them) and which can be launched by clicking on its icon, which appears on the Desktop and also in the Main Menu. Within File Station they can see the folders and files that belong to them or to which they have been granted access, such as their home folder and any shared folders.

To work with a file or folder, right-click it and a pop-up menu will appear with the various available options. Alternatively, highlight it and click the **Action** button:

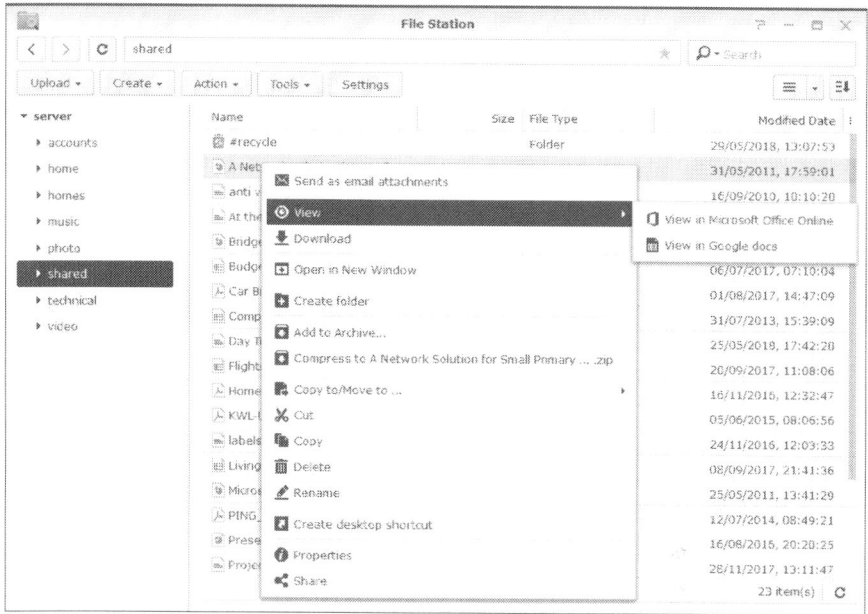

Figure 27: Using File Station

There are options to view documents, spreadsheets and presentations using *Google Docs*, Microsoft *Office Online* or *Synology Office* (if installed - see section **6 SYNOLOGY DRIVE & OFFICE**). If it is required to edit a file, choose the **Download** option to first download it to the local computer. Make the changes to the document using Word, Excel or other preferred application, then use the **Upload** button in File Station to upload the new version back to the server. Most graphic files and photographs can be viewed by double-clicking them and from there they can be zoomed and manipulated. MP3 music files can be played. There are also common file manipulation commands for copying, renaming, deleting files and so on.

When the user has finished, they should logout. To this, click on the **Options** icon in the top right-corner of the screen depicting a human head and shoulders and choose **Logout**:

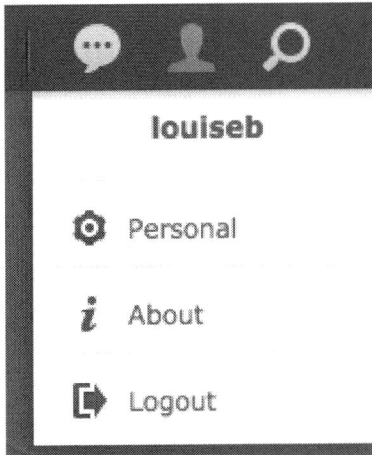

Figure 28: Options icon

5.2 Using Windows Explorer/File Explorer

A simple way to access the server directly is by going into Windows Explorer (called File Explorer in Windows 8/8.1/10). Expand the left-hand panel to view the Network and down the left-hand side the server should be visible. Click on it and the list of shared folders will be displayed:

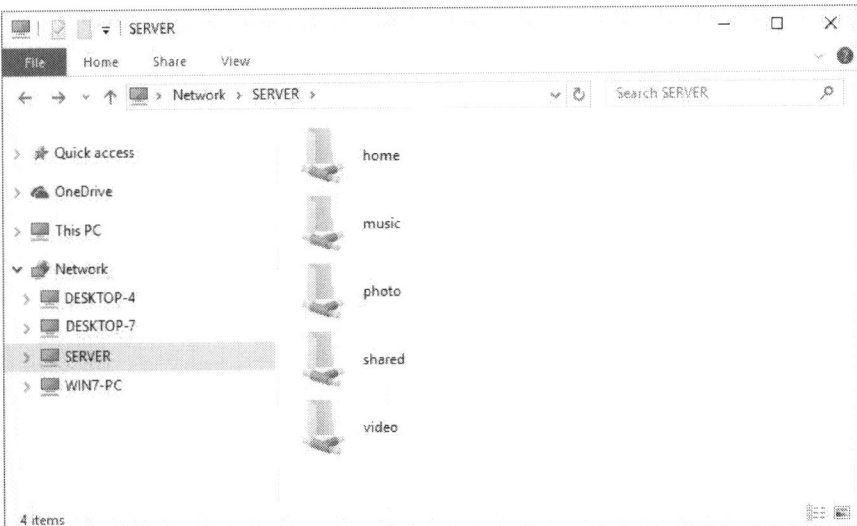

Figure 29: List of folders from Windows Explorer/File Explorer

To access a shared folder, double-click it – you will be prompted to enter a user name and password as defined previously on the server. If you wish, tick the option box to remember the login details, although you should only do this if you are the sole user of the computer. Although many shared folders may be visible, you can only access the ones to which you have privileges.

5.3 Accessing Shared Folders Using the Run Command

To access a shared folder from a Windows computer, click **Start** then choose **Run** (in the case of Windows 8.1 and Windows 10, right-click the **Start** button then choose **Run**). Alternatively, hold down the **Windows key** and press the letter **R**. In the small dialog box that appears, type in the name of the shared folder using the format \\server\name_of_folder e.g. \\server\shared then click **OK**.

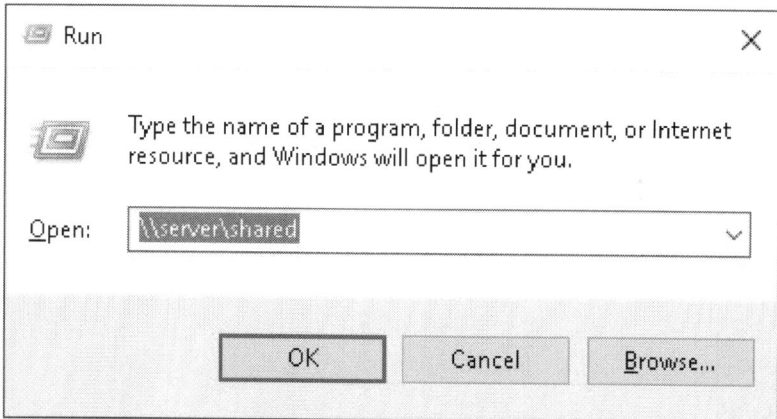

Figure 30: Accessing a shared folder

The contents of the folder will be displayed in Windows Explorer/File Explorer, from where the files can be used in the standard way. Note that you may be prompted to enter a user name and password as defined previously on the server.

5.4 Mapping Drives Manually

The techniques considered so far provide access to shared folders by referring to them using what are called UNC or *Universal Naming Convention* names, which take the form of *server**shared*. However, many Windows users are accustomed to and prefer to use drive letters, such as C:, D: and so on. The process by which a UNC name can be turned into a drive letter is known as *mapping* and there are several ways to go about, discussed in the following sections.

Network drives can be mapped manually using Windows Explorer/File Explorer on the user's PC. The first stage of the process is slightly different, depending on the version of Windows, so check the relevant version below then jump to the common 'Map Network Drive' section underneath.

Windows 10

Open File Explorer, which usually appears on the Taskbar by default. Expand the left-hand panel to view the Network and click on the server to display the list of shared folders. Note: you may be prompted to enter a valid user name and password as previously defined on the server. If you wish, tick the option box to remember the login details, although you should only do this if you are the sole user of the computer. Right-click on the shared folder to highlight it. On the menu bar click **Home** and in the *New* section click the small icon and choose **Map as drive**:

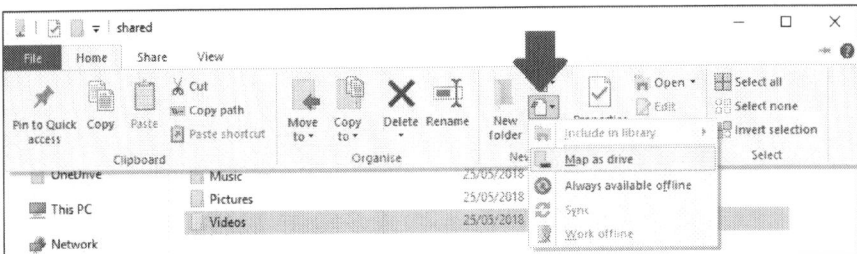

Figure 31: Map as drive in Windows 10

—

58

Windows 8.1

If using Windows 8 or 8.1 open File Explorer, which usually appears on the Taskbar by default. On the menu bar click **This PC** then click the **Map network drive icon** on the ribbon, followed by **Map network drive** on the dropdown.

Windows 7

If using Windows 7 open Windows Explorer, which usually appears on the Taskbar by default, else click **My Computer** on the Start menu. If the menu bar is not displayed, click **Organize > Layout > Menu bar** to display it. From the Menu bar choose **Tools > Map Network Drive**.

Windows Vista

If using Windows Vista run Windows Explorer by clicking **Start > All Programs > Accessories > Windows Explorer**, else click Computer on the **Start** menu. If the menu bar is not displayed, click **Organize > Layout > Menu bar** to display it. From the Menu bar choose **Tools > Map Network Drive**.

Windows XP

If using Windows XP run Windows Explorer by clicking **Start > All Programs > Accessories > Windows Explorer**, else click **My Computer** on the **Start** menu. From the menu bar choose **Tools > Map Network Drive**.

Map Network Drive

On the resultant panel choose a drive letter from the drop-down. For the Folder, click on the **Browse** button and navigate through the network to find the server and the desired folder. Alternatively, just type in the name of the folder. If the computer is only ever used by one person tick the **Reconnect at sign-in** box – this will cause Windows to remember the mapping.

Then click **Finish**. You may be prompted to enter the user's name and password that were defined earlier on the DiskStation. Again, if the computer is used just by one person tick the **Remember my credentials** box. Then click **OK**.

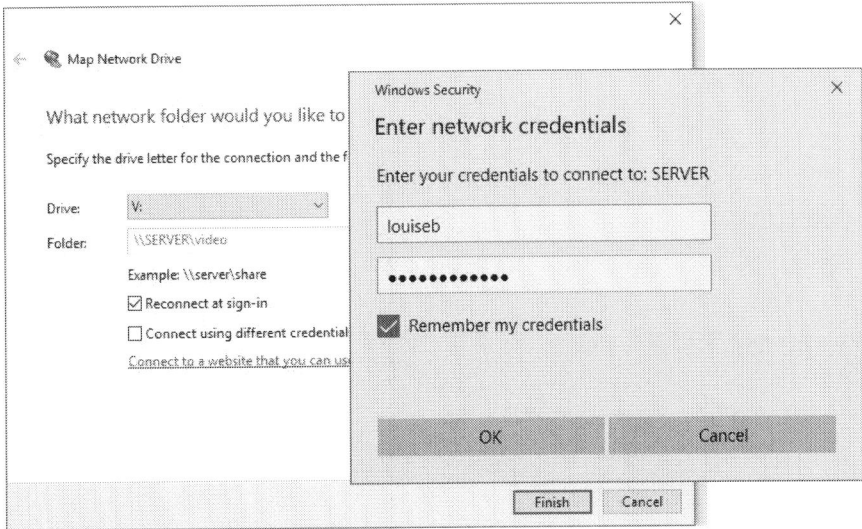

Figure 32: Mapping a drive

Upon a successful connection, the contents of the newly mapped drive will be displayed. The process should now be repeated for each folder that the user needs access to.

You can use whatever drive letters you wish, as long as they are not already in use (for instance you cannot use C as that is always in use on a Windows computer). However, using sensible letters makes things easier. For example, map *music* to M, *photo* to P and *video* to V. Here are some suggested mappings:

Drive	Folder
H	\\server\home
M	\\server\music
P	\\server\photo
S	\\server\shared
V	\\server\video

5.5 Using Synology Assistant

The Synology Assistant is a flexible piece of software that can do several different things, one of which is mapping drives. One possible advantage of using it is consistency; when drives are mapped manually in Windows as described in the previous section there are small variations in the process depending on what version of Windows is being used. However, using the Synology Assistant it is the same process regardless of the Windows version. Mac and Linux versions of Synology Assistant is available, but do not map drives and so are not discussed here.

Download and install the Synology Assistant on each computer. If you receive a message from the computer's firewall, grant the Synology Assistant access. An icon will be placed on the computer's desktop – double-click it to run it. The following window is displayed:

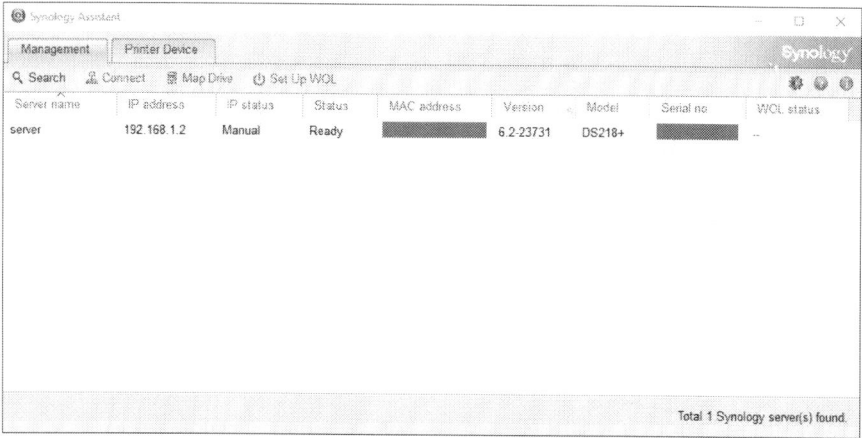

Figure 33: Finding the server using the Synology Assistant

The server should be listed, although the Synology Assistant may take a few seconds to find it. If it does not appear click the **Search** button; if it still does not appear then there is a problem of some sort, such as: computer not connected to network; DiskStation not powered on; firewall needs configuring on computer. Click on the server entry – it will then become possible to click the **Map Drive** button. Do so and you will be prompted to enter logon details for the user. Then click **Next**:

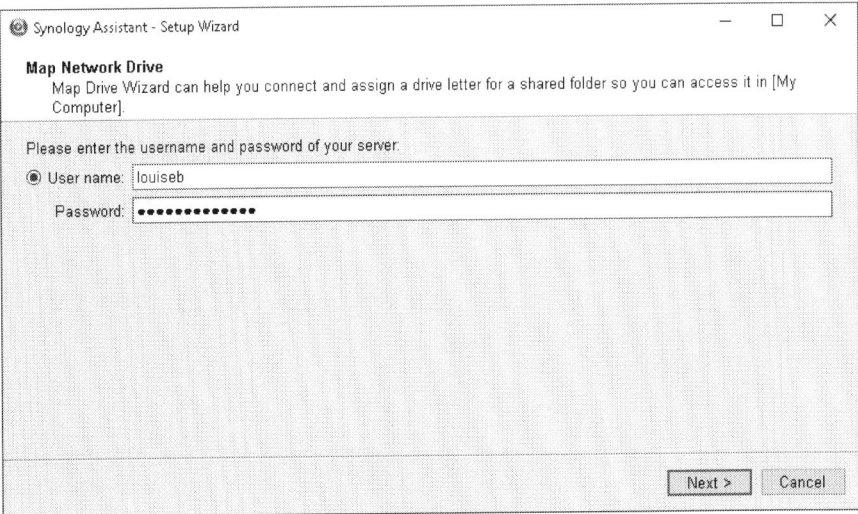

Figure 34: Enter user name and password

The subsequent screen shows the folders to which the user has access. Choose a folder and click **Next**. On the subsequent screen choose a drive letter for the folder from the drop-down; the default is Z but you can use any free letter. If the computer is only ever used by one person you can tick the **Reconnect at logon** box, then click **Next**.

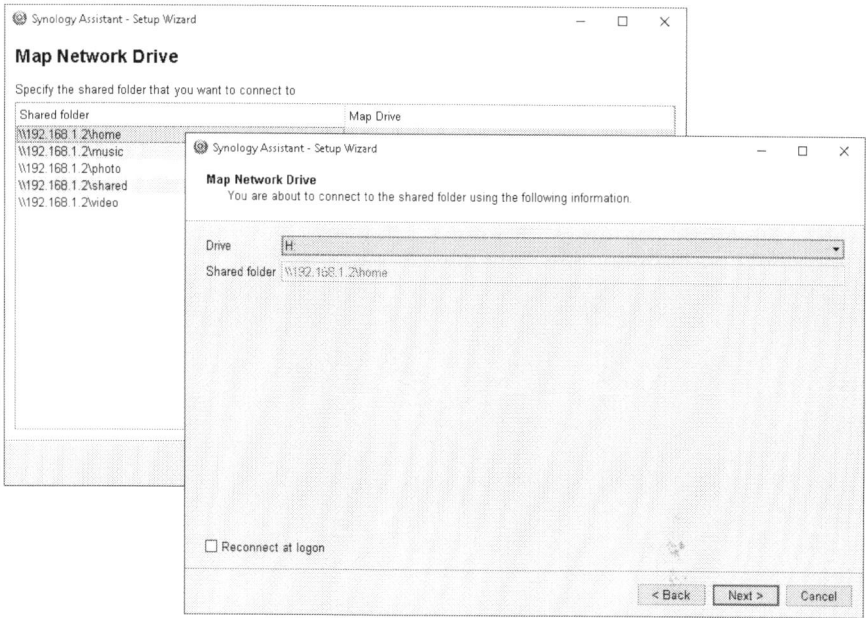

Figure 35: Mapping a network drive

You may receive an additional logon prompt from Windows, in which case enter the login details, tick the **Remember my credentials** box if only one person uses the computer, followed by **OK**. The drive will then be mapped – click **Finish** on the confirmation screen. Repeat the process for as many times as is necessary to provide access to all the desired folders. When complete, close the Synology Assistant (in fact, it will continue to run on the Taskbar unless explicitly shutdown) and open Windows Explorer/File Explorer to verify that the folders have been mapped to drives.

Note that the drive mappings are permanent - assuming the **Reconnect at logon** and **Remember my credentials** boxes were ticked - and hence will survive reboots of the computer. It is not necessary to run the Synology Assistant again unless it is required to make changes to the mappings.

As stated, you can use whatever drive letters you wish, as long as they are not already in use (for instance you cannot use C as that is always allocated on a Windows computer). However, using sensible letters makes things easier. For example, map *music* to M, *photo* to P and *video* to V. Here are some suggested mappings:

Drive	Folder
H	\\server\home
M	\\server\music
P	\\server\photo
S	\\server\shared
V	\\server\video

5.6 Connecting Macs

There are numerous iterations of the Mac operating system and some minor differences between them; however, the following technique should work with all versions. Modern versions of macOS use the same SMB protocol as Windows, but nevertheless it is suggested that AFP (the Mac File Service) is enabled on the DiskStation; this is the default on a new DSM installation but can be verified by going to the **Control Panel** and checking **File Services** (also see section **2.5 File Services**).

On the menu bar of the Mac, click **Go** followed by **Connect to Server**. Alternatively, press **Command K**. A dialog box is displayed. Enter the name or IP address of the DiskStation, preceded with the characters *smb://*. If you have difficulties or are using an old version of OS X then try preceding the name or IP address with the characters *afp://*

e.g. *192.168.1.2* or *afp://192.168.1.2* or *afp://server*

To add the server to your list of Favorites for future reference click the **+** button. Then click **Connect**:

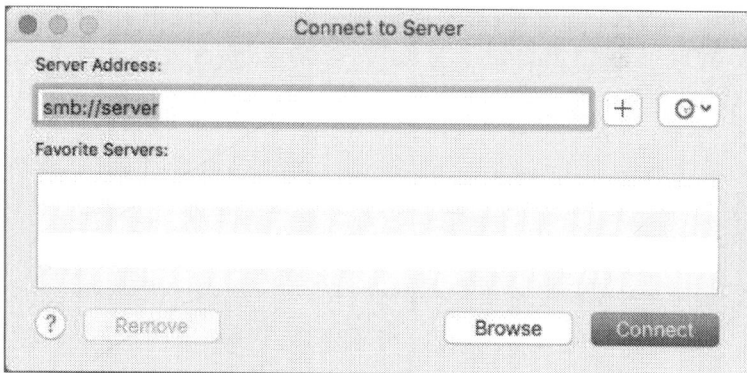

Figure 36: Specifying the address of the server

Specify the user name and password as defined on the DiskStation (**not** the local Mac user name) and click **Connect**:

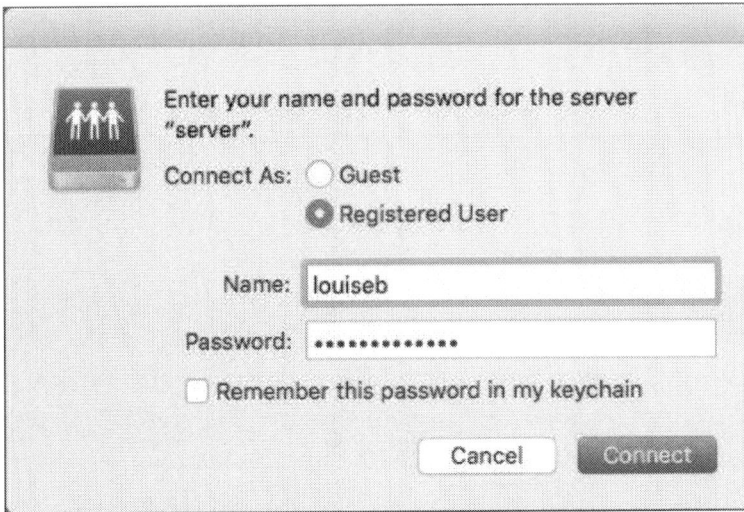

Figure 37: Enter the user name and password

A list of shared folders is displayed, referred to as *volumes* in Apple parlance. Choose the volume to mount and click **OK**. Note: to mount multiple volumes in one go, hold down the **Command key** and click on the required folders in turn. Icon(s) for the folder(s) will appear on the Desktop (assuming you have set Preferences in Finder to show Connected Servers). Click an icon to display the contents - they behave exactly the same as standard Mac folders.

A slight variation on the above is to click on the Mac's hard drive icon on the Desktop (if set to show), navigate to the Server (DiskStation), click the **Connect** button and then login and mount one or more volumes (shared folders).

5.7 Smartphones & Tablets

There are several different methods for connecting smartphones and tablets to DiskStations. All involve downloadable apps, but they meet different needs and are complementary rather than exclusive. The first method comprises apps that provide direct access to the files on the server, and is the focus of this section. The second method involves Synology Drive, which enables files to be synchronized between devices and the server using the internet and is discussed in chapter **6 SYNOLOGY DRIVE & OFFICE**.

DS File

The simplest method to gain access is with *DS File,* which is a free download from Synology and is available for iOS and Android from the respective App stores. Download, install and launch DS File on the portable device; enter the QuickConnect ID or IP address of the server, along with the user name and password. It is then possible to navigate the filing system and open documents using the built-in file viewers. Files can be downloaded to and from the device and printed if you have a compatible printer. There are also basic commands for manipulating files.

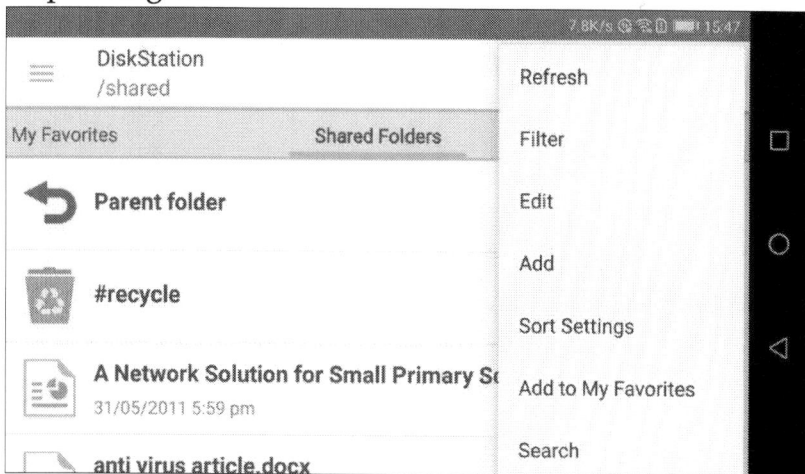

Figure 38: Viewing a folder using DS File on Android phone

5.8 Connecting Linux Computers

Although DSM includes comprehensive support for the NFS filing system used by Linux and UNIX computers (see **2.5 File Services**), most Linux distributions include support for the SMB filing system used by DSM. Unless you have specific reason not to, it is suggested that you use SMB for connecting. The ability to do this is either built-in, or can be added by downloading what is commonly described as a Samba client.

In this example, we are using the popular Ubuntu Linux distribution.

On the Linux computer, click on the **Files** icon, followed by **Connect to Server**. In the resultant dialog box, enter the address of the DiskStation preceded by *smb://* e.g. *smb://192.168.1.2* and click **Connect**:

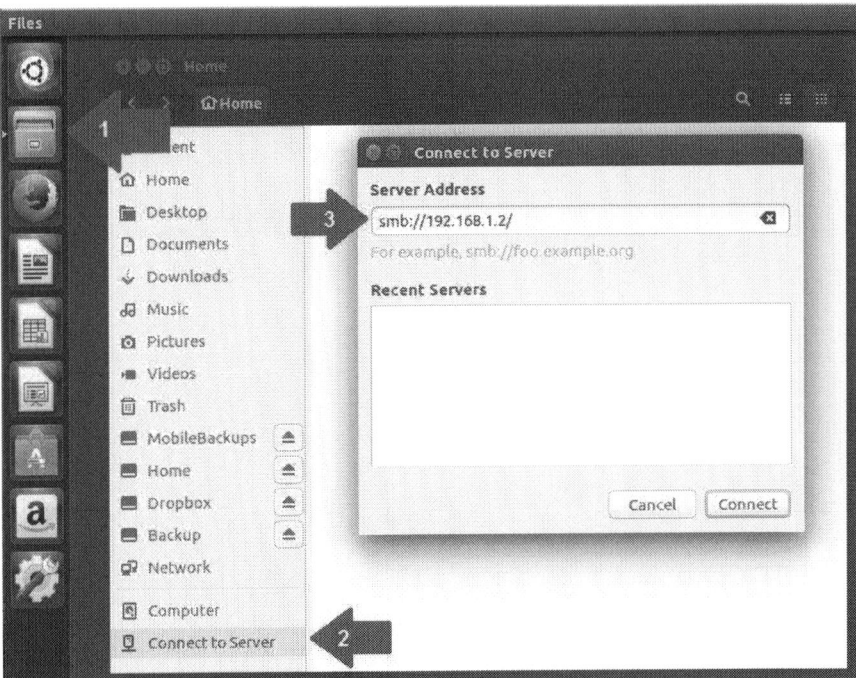

Figure 39: Enter the address of the server

On the resultant panel, enter the user's name and password as defined on the server and click **Connect** (the *Domain* field can be ignored):

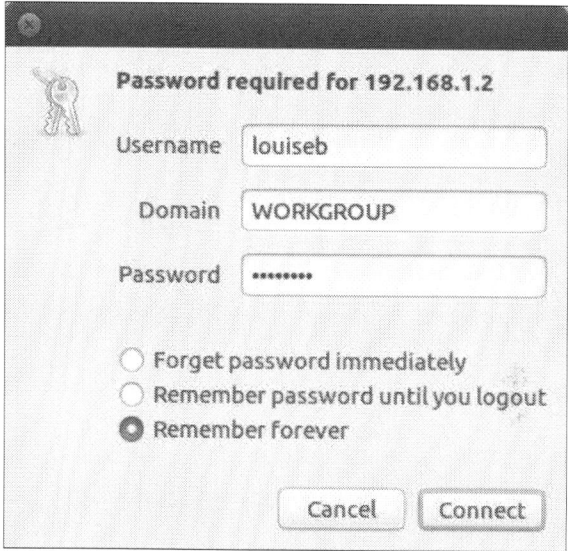

Figure 40: Enter the user's details

The shared folders on the server will be listed. To access one, double-click on it. You may be prompted to provide the username and password again, in which case do so. The folder will then open and you can use the files in the normal manner.

6 SYNOLOGY DRIVE & OFFICE

6.1 Overview of Synology Drive

Most people will be familiar with cloud-based services such as Dropbox, OneDrive, Google Drive, iCloud and so on. The basic idea is simple: somewhere on the internet is an amount of private space for your usage – think of it as like a USB memory stick or hard drive in the sky. Data stored on the cloud can be accessed in two ways: the first method is by logging in to the website and working within a browser; the second method is to have a folder on your computer or device corresponding to that space, along with client software or an app. Anything you put in that folder is automatically copied ('synced') to the space on the internet, or vice versa: whenever anything changes on one computer, the change is reflected automatically on the other.

Some cloud services specialize in providing provide storage (for example, Dropbox), whereas others also include tools for creating and editing documents (for instance, Microsoft Office Online/OneDrive and Google Docs/Drive). Whilst incredibly useful and deservedly popular, these services do have some limitations. Firstly, although they usually give some free space, it may not be very much and if you need more you have to pay for it e.g. Dropbox gives 2GB free but charges US $119.88 / UK £95.98 a year for 1TB. Secondly, most services have restrictions on file sizes and how much data you can store on them. Finally, some people are just not comfortable with the idea of their data being held by Microsoft or Google or whoever. *Synology Drive & Office* get round all of these issues: they are free to obtain and use; there are no practical restrictions on space and usage; data is stored on your own server, meaning everything is under your control.

Put simply – they are a private alternative to Google and Microsoft etc and particularly suitable for people who travel away from home or the office where their DiskStation is located.

Strictly speaking, Drive and Office are separate packages. If you just wanted cloud storage and did not require word processing, spreadsheet and presentation features, you could just install Drive. However, they are so closely related and integrated that it usually makes sense to install both and that is what we will do.

6.2 Installing & Configuring Synology Drive & Office

Synology Drive uses QuickConnect, so if you have not already done so, setup a QuickConnect ID as described in section **2.7 QuickConnect: The Key to Remote Connectivity**. You may have chosen to install Synology Drive during the initial installation of DSM, else download and install it from the Package Center. It requires Synology Application Service and some other components and these will also be installed if not already in place, so installation may take several minutes. The installation process places two icons in the Main Menu: *Drive Admin Console*, for administering the facility, and *Drive* for using the system. Next, download and install *Office* from the Package Center; when you do so, you may again be advised that some additional components need to be downloaded and installed – this is fine, so click **Yes** to continue. Installation will take several minutes.

After installation is complete, launch **Drive Admin Console** from the Main Menu. Provided it has picked up your QuickConnect ID, it will enable itself and display the following panel:

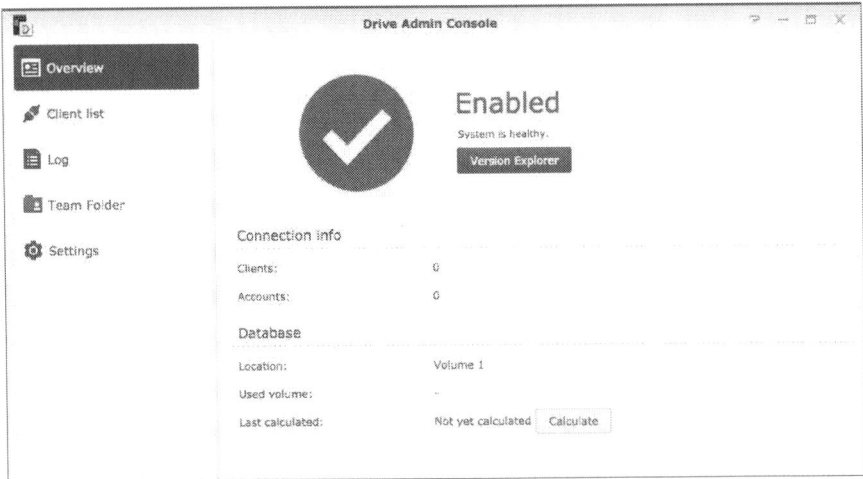

Figure 41: Drive Admin Console

Individual users need to be given permission to use *Drive*; to do so, go to **Control Panel > User**, highlight a name and click **Edit**. On the *Applications* tab, tick the **Allow** box for *Drive*, followed by **OK**. Suggestion: if you have many users who need access to Drive, consider creating a specific group for them and then grant application permissions to that group. If you want everyone to have access to it, give application permissions to the built-in *users* group instead.

The default behaviour is that each authorized user will have a personal Drive folder created inside their individual Home folder on the server. If this is sufficient for your needs, then proceed to the following sections. However, if you want or need to share additional folders, there is the ability to setup so-called *Team Folders*. Click on the **Team Folder** tab, which will display a list of shared folders on the server. To use a folder with Drive, highlight it then click the **Enable** button. Avoid the temptation to share everything: in this example it is just the folder called *shared* that will be synced. Click **OK** on the panel that is displayed; note the warning message that users must have full read/write access to the shared folder(s), otherwise the synchronization will be in one direction only i.e. from the server to the computer:

72

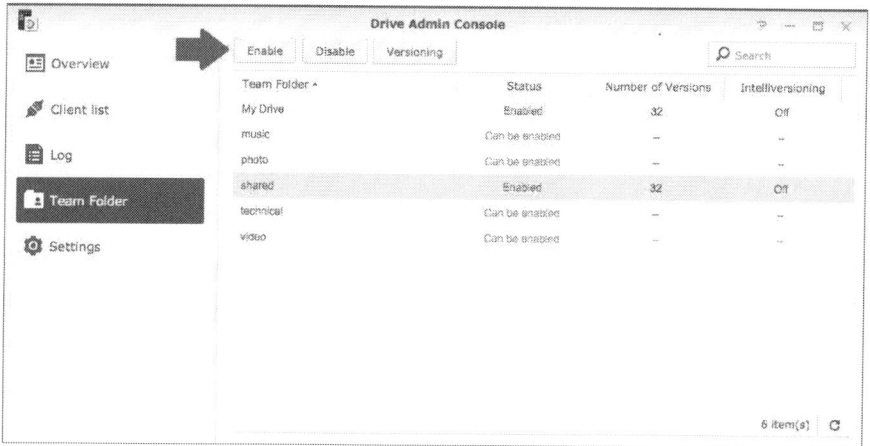

Figure 42: Choosing a Team Folder

There are three other tabs: the **Client List** and **Log** tabs enable you to monitor who is using Drive and how. The **Settings** tab enables fine control over many aspects of Drive, but in a typical home or small business environment you probably will not have to worry about it as the default settings are fine in most scenarios.

Returning to the **Overview** screen, there is a blue button marked **Version Explorer**. This enables older versions of synced files to be recovered and manipulated in the event of problems, such as users deleting files accidentally.

6.3 Accessing Drive with a Browser

The easiest method to access *Drive* is using a browser, as it requires no additional software to be installed on the user's device. The user should login to the server, as described in section **5.1 Using a Browser**. From the **Main Menu**, click **Drive**, which will cause it to open in a new browser tab:

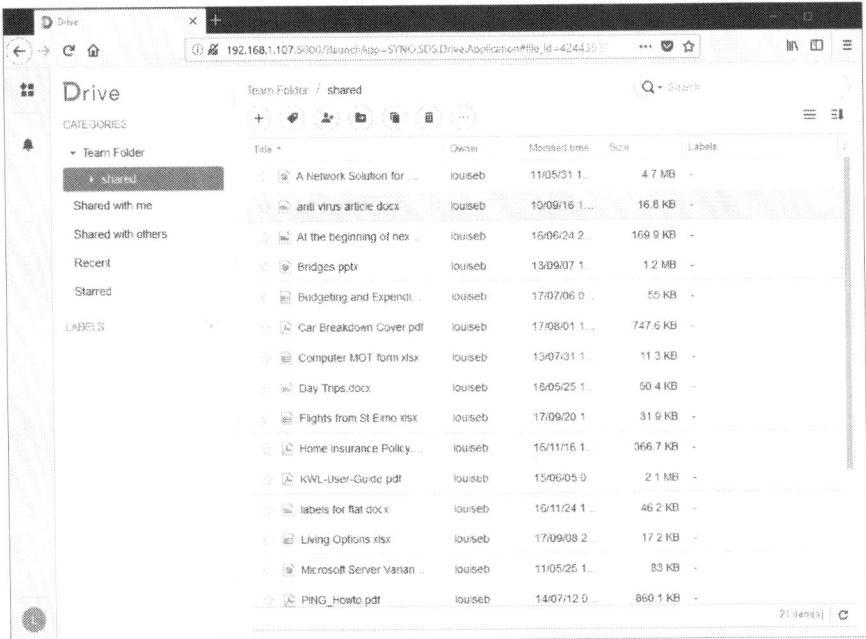

Figure 43: Drive, as viewed from a browser

The folders and categories to which the user has access are listed down the left-hand side of the screen, with the contents of the current location listed in the right-hand panel. If a file is right-clicked, a pop-up menu with a list of options is displayed; this includes many file manipulation commands such as Copy, Delete, Rename and so on. A limited selection of files can be viewed by double-clicking them.

To work with a file on the computer using a locally installed application such as Word or Excel etc., right-click it and choose **Download** from the pop-up menu; the edited file can then be uploaded back into Drive.

When the user has finished using Drive, they should logout by clicking on their initial or photo in the bottom left-hand corner of the screen.

6.4 Desktop Drive Client

For many people, accessing Drive using a browser will seem cumbersome and they would much prefer to access data in the same way as they do with local files on their computer. This can be done using the client synchronization software or Desktop Drive Client, which is available from the Download Center section of the Synology website for Windows, Mac and Linux. All versions look and behave in a very similar manner.

Upon running the Drive client for the first time, click **Start Now** and on the following screen enter the *QuickConnect ID* name that was registered with Synology, the *Username* and *Password*, then click **Next**. If a warning message about the SSL Certificate is given, click **Proceed Anyway**:

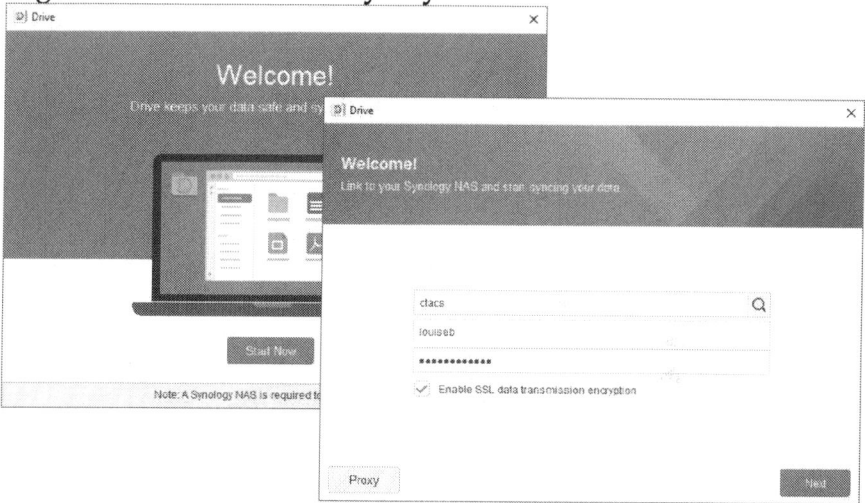

Figure 44: Setting up the Drive client

The next screen shows the folders to be synchronized. The default is that a folder in the user computer's home folder, called *SynologyDrive*, will be synced with a folder called *Drive* in the user's home folder on the server. This will suit most people, but if you wanted to change the folders for some reason, you can do so by clicking on the 'pencil' icons. You can also fine-tune the syncing process through use of the **Advanced** button. Click **Next**:

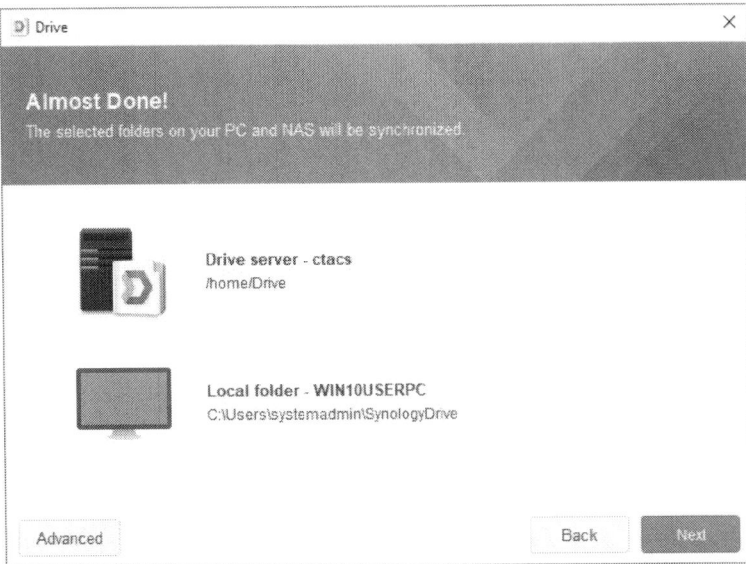

Figure 45: Specify the folder to be synchronized

The subsequent screen allows additional files and folders shared by others to be synced to the user's computer, where they can be edited locally. By default, Synology suggest you enable this feature, but we suggest you take the **Maybe later** option to reduce confusion. Click **Done**.

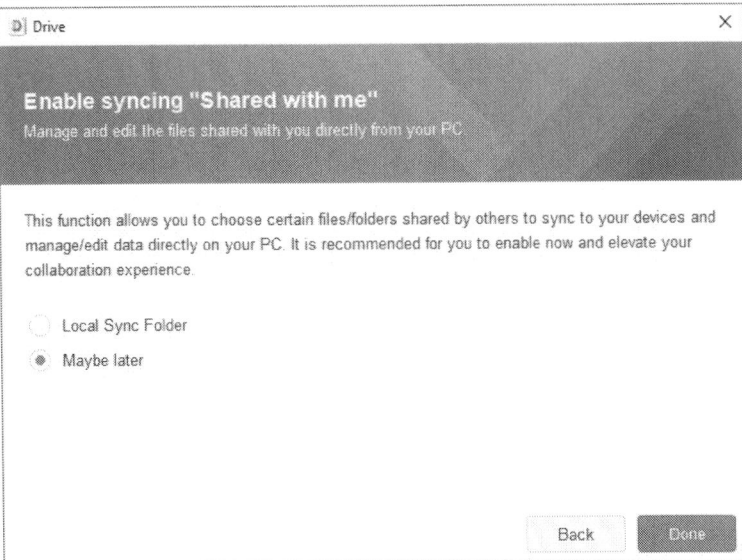

Figure 46: Optional, additional syncing

That is it. Anything placed in the *SynologyDrive* folder on the computer – which is just a standard folder as far as the computer is concerned - will automatically be synchronized with the server (and vice versa). On a Windows PC, an icon for the local Drive folder is placed on the Desktop for convenience; double-click to open then simply drag files into it. On Mac, the SynologyDrive folder is located in the user's work space e.g. for a user called *louiseb* it would be */Users/louiseb/SynologyDrive* (if you navigate to this location in Finder you can make an alias for it and place it on the Desktop). In the case of Linux, it is necessary to manually locate the desired folder on the computer, referred to as the backup source (the pencil icons for navigating within the client are not present).

An icon is also placed on the Menu bar (Mac) or Task bar (Windows), which can be used for monitoring Synology Drive. There is a small menu bar in the bottom right-hand corner which can be used for fine-tuning the options and adding or modifying synchronization tasks.

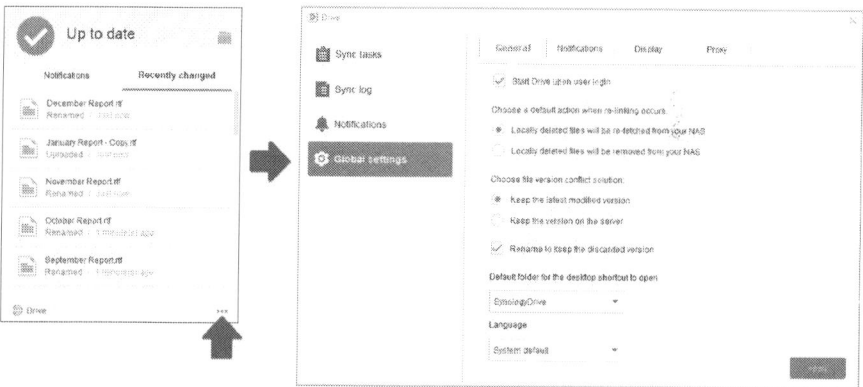

Figure 47: Drive client settings

6.5 Mobile Drive Client

Synology provide a mobile Drive client, available from the respective app stores for iOS and Android smartphones and tablets. When running it for the first time, it is necessary to configure it by specifying the QuickConnect ID, user name and password, plus it is suggested that you enable the HTTPS switch. The screen then appears, along the following lines:

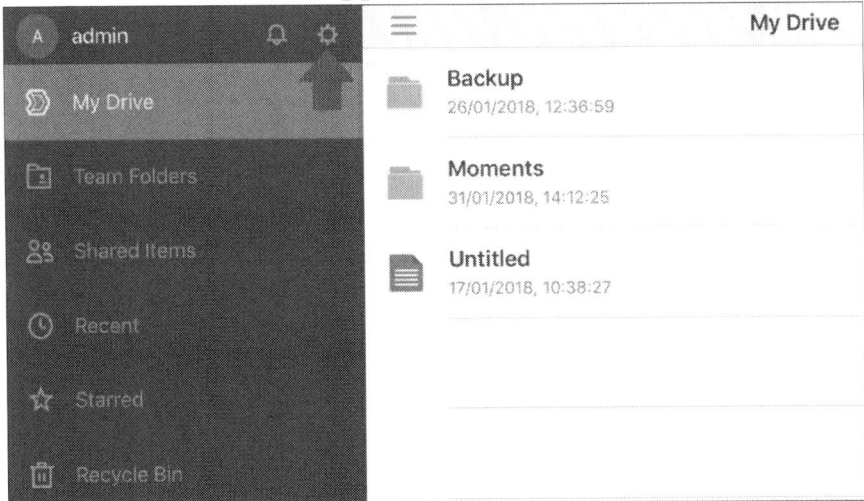

Figure 48: Drive client running on iPhone

The mobile client is possibly best considered as a means for viewing folders and files stored on the DiskStation. However, it can also be used for uploading files, folders and photographs from the mobile device to the server.

The default settings in the client will be suitable for most people and purposes. However, there is one parameter that you may wish to change. Typically, a user may have a lot more data stored in Drive on the DiskStation than will fit on their smartphone or tablet. To cope with this, plus improve overall performance, the mobile Drive client only maintains the most recently used data locally, via a so-called *cache*. If the device has a relatively small amount of local storage, say, 8GB, then you may wish to minimize the size of the cache.

Conversely, if the device has a relatively large amount of storage e.g. 128GB, then you may wish to increase the size of the cache. To do, click the settings wheel (indicated by the arrow in the above screenshot), click **Cache management** and choose a value.

6.6 Using Office

To use Office, a user should login to the server using a browser as described in section **5.1 Using a Browser**. They will not have a specific icon for Office; rather, the way it is implemented is by adding capabilities to Drive. The icon for Drive can be found on the user's **Main Menu** and clicking it will launch Drive in a new tab. There are two main changes: firstly, a far wider variety of files (e.g. spreadsheets and documents) can now by viewed and edited by double-clicking them. Secondly, clicking the plus sign button (+) displays a pop-up menu with seven options: create a folder; create a word processing document; create a spreadsheet; create a presentation; create a document using a built-in template (Synology provide around two dozen, suitable for many common tasks); create an encrypted file i.e. a document or spreadsheet encrypted with a password; add additional files:

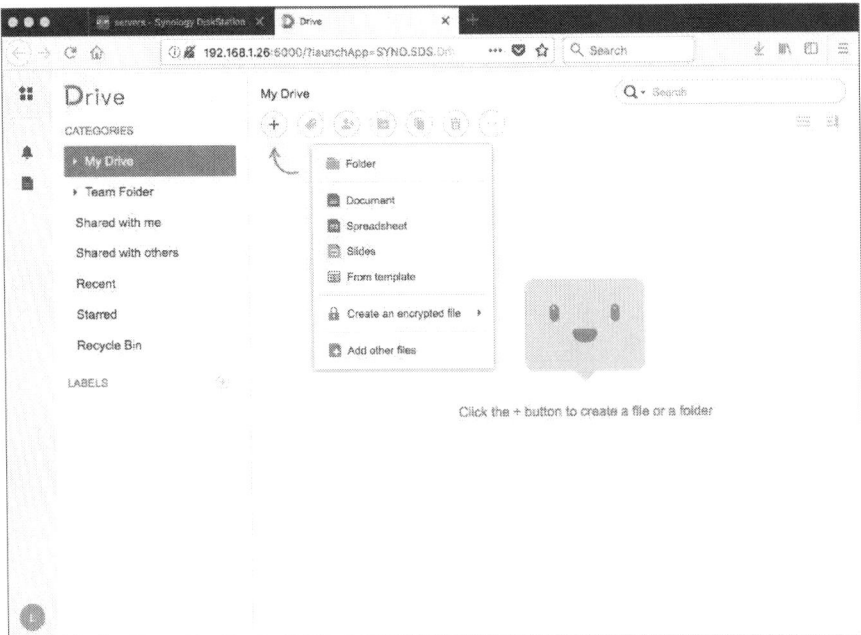

Figure 49: The opening screen for Office

The word processor, spreadsheet and presentation program are largely conventional in operation and behave much as might be expected, although are somewhat simpler than, say, regular Microsoft Word, Excel and PowerPoint. One thing to note is that files do not have to explicitly be saved, as saving happens automatically.

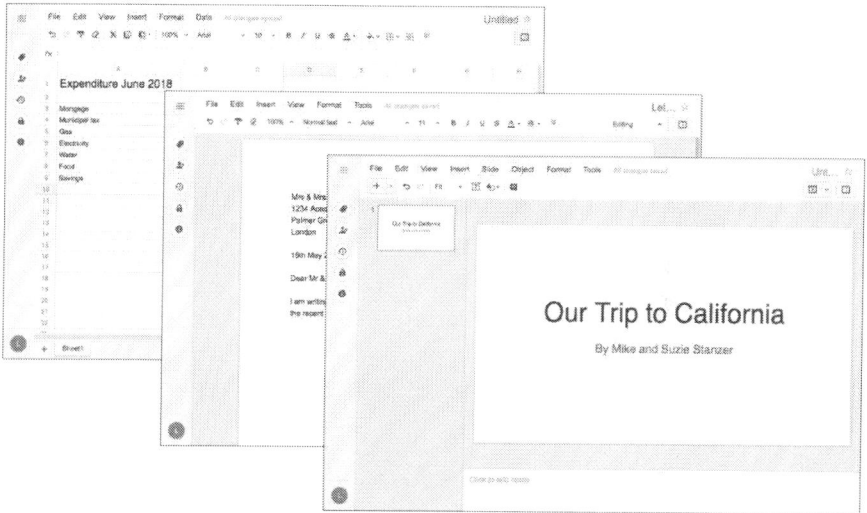

Figure 50: Spreadsheets, documents and presentations in Office

Synology Office is intended as a collaborative tool and to this end there is the ability to share files, with other local DSM users on the network or the world at large. Files can be shared at any stage, from within the user's main screen or whilst editing, using the **File Share** command.

When finished, the user can logout by clicking their initial or photograph in the bottom left-hand corner of the screen and choosing the **Logout** option.

7 BACKUPS

It is extremely important to backup data on a regular basis, in order to cope with the problems that can arise with computers. Examples of things that can go wrong include: deleting files by accident; virus and malware infections; data corruption; computer failure; equipment being lost or stolen. In general, the value of data far outweighs the value of computers; for instance, what price could be attached to the irreplaceable photos of a Wedding day, children's first steps or other important occasion? In the case of businesses, around half that have a serious data loss subsequently cease trading within twelve months, plus there may be statutory requirements to retain certain data and be able to produce it in some parts of the world. The assumption to follow is that it is a question of *when* rather than *if* data will be lost at some point, which is when the backups will be needed.

Backups are a bit like pay rises or happy memories – you cannot have too many of them. A NAS system such as a DiskStation forms the ideal heart of any backup solution and enables you to take a multi-tiered approach. Basically that means there are multiple backups to multiple places, ensuring that there is always a fallback plan in the event of problems. For example:
The computers in the home or office are backed up to the NAS. The NAS in turn is backed up to a local USB hard drive. Optionally, the NAS or at least the most important data are backed up to a Cloud-based service. In the case of a slightly larger business, the NAS may also be backed up to a second NAS located on or off the premises:

1. Computers back up to NAS

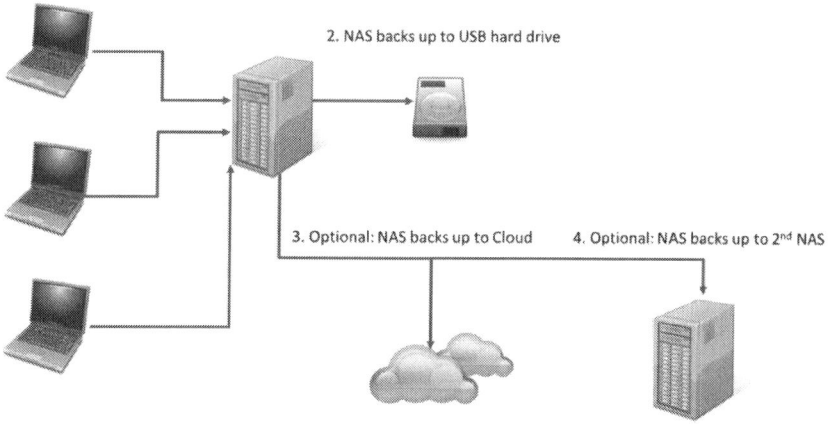

2. NAS backs up to USB hard drive

3. Optional: NAS backs up to Cloud   4. Optional: NAS backs up to 2nd NAS

Figure 51: Example of multi-tier backup

DSM has provision for all these types of backup. Numerous backup apps are available from Synology and third parties, but the standard one is Synology's own *Hyper Backup*. Depending on the options chosen, this may have been downloaded and installed during the installation of DSM. If not, it can be downloaded from the Package Center (for general information see **9.1 Package Center**).

The most common scenario is to backup the DiskStation to an external drive so this is what we will concentrate on first. As an additional level of backup, consider using a cloud service as described in section **7.3 Backing Up Using Cloud Services**.

7.1 Backing Up the DiskStation to an External Drive

This backup solution requires an external hard drive, which we will assume this to be a USB drive, although some DiskStations also support eSATA drives. The drive should be: USB 3.0 specification (USB 2.0 drives will work but are slower); of sufficient capacity to hold all the data but preferably larger (for example if there is 2TB data then use at least a 2TB drive but a 3TB drive would be better still); portable if possible, as they do not require mains power and are more convenient to store. To prepare for backup usage, plug the drive into a spare USB socket on the DiskStation. Note that on some DiskStations not all of the USB sockets are of USB 3.0 specification.

Click **Control Panel** followed by **External Devices**. The drive should appear after a few seconds; highlight it and click **Format**. Choose to format the **Entire disk**, using DSM's preferred file system type of **EXT4**. Click **OK** and acknowledge the warning message that is displayed. The formatting may take some time, depending on the capacity and speed of the drive. It is suggested that you do this step, regardless of whether the drive is a new, blank one, or one that was purchased pre-formatted as often such drives will have been pre-formatted with the Windows exFAT or NTFS filing systems, which are unsuitable:

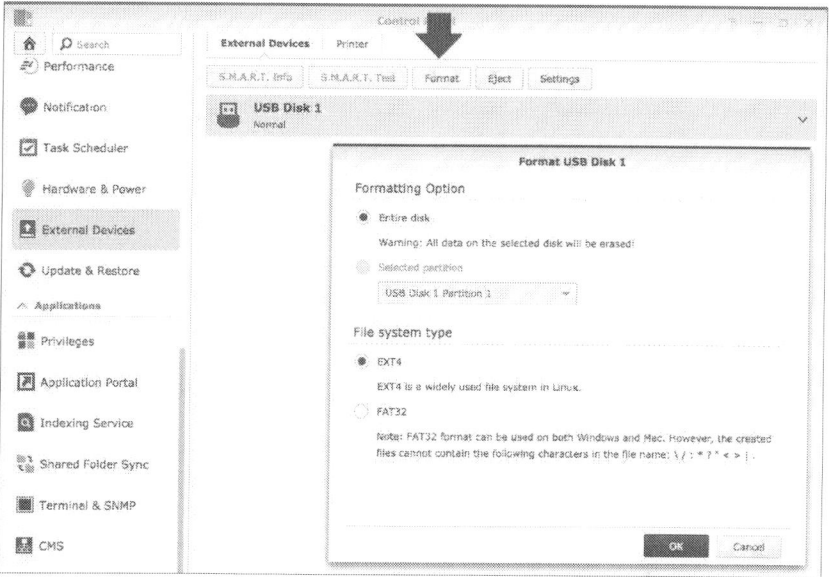

Figure 52: Format external backup drive

When the external drive has been formatted, quit External Devices, go to the **Main Menu** and launch **Hyper Backup**, which will display the following screen the first time it is run:

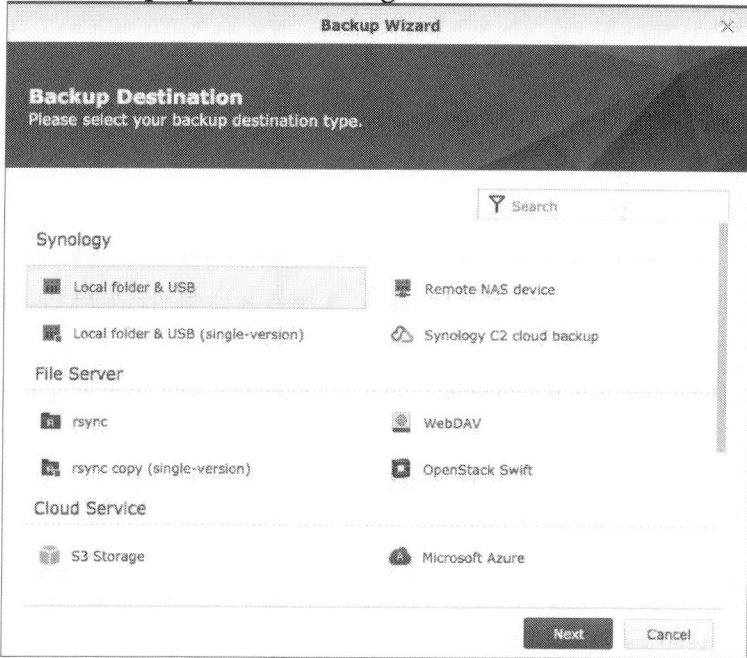

Figure 53: Choose backup destination type

Start by specifying a *Backup Destination*: there are many options to choose from, but for backing up to a USB drive, highlight *Local Shared Folder & USB* and click **Next**. On the follow-on screen, choose **Create backup task** and from the *Shared Folder* drop-down select the external backup drive, which is *usbshare1* in our example. The *Directory* entry is unimportant, so just click **Next**:

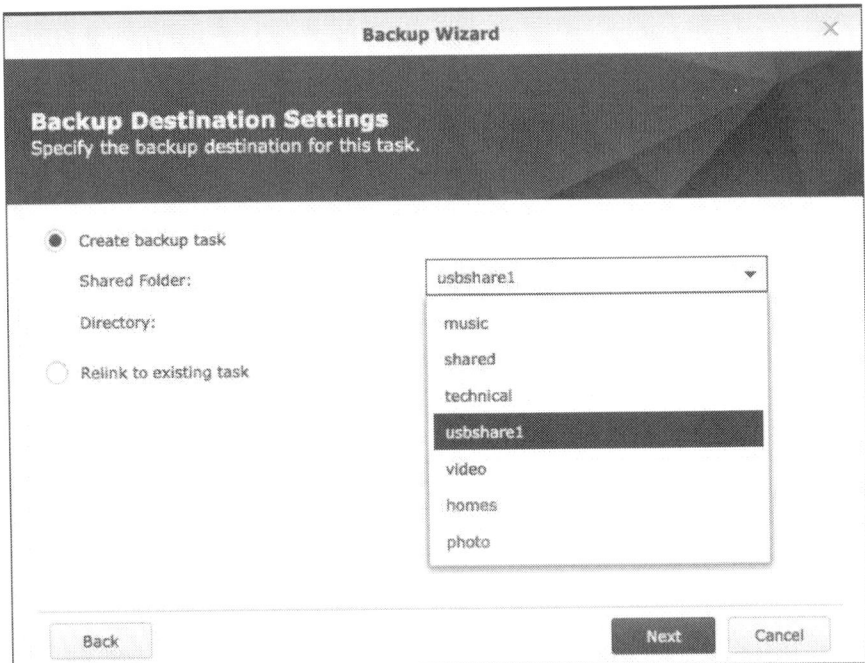

Figure 54: Specify the backup destination

On the next screen, choose the folders to be backed up. The most common requirement is to backup everything, so tick all the folders followed by click **Next**:

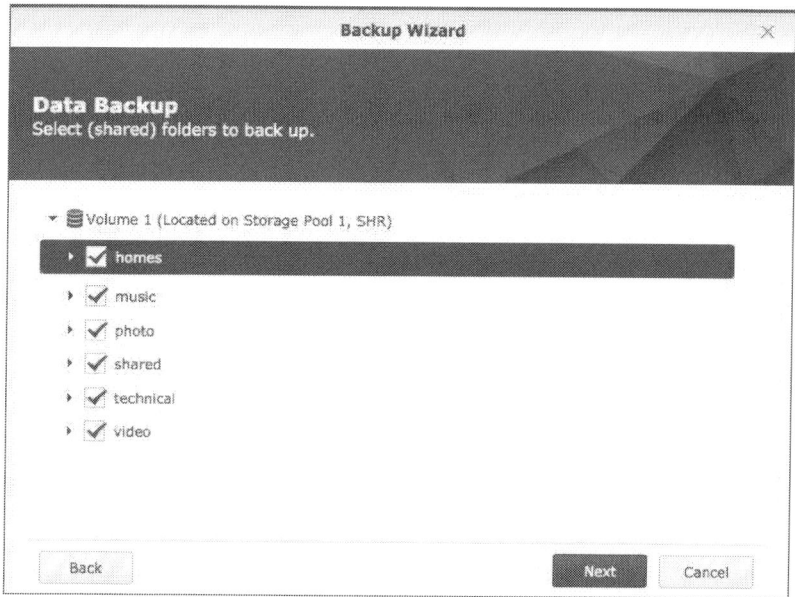

Figure 55: Select folders to be backed up

If you have installed applications from the Package Center that store their own data, you may receive a screen that allows you to include them into the backup. Select as appropriate and click **Next**:

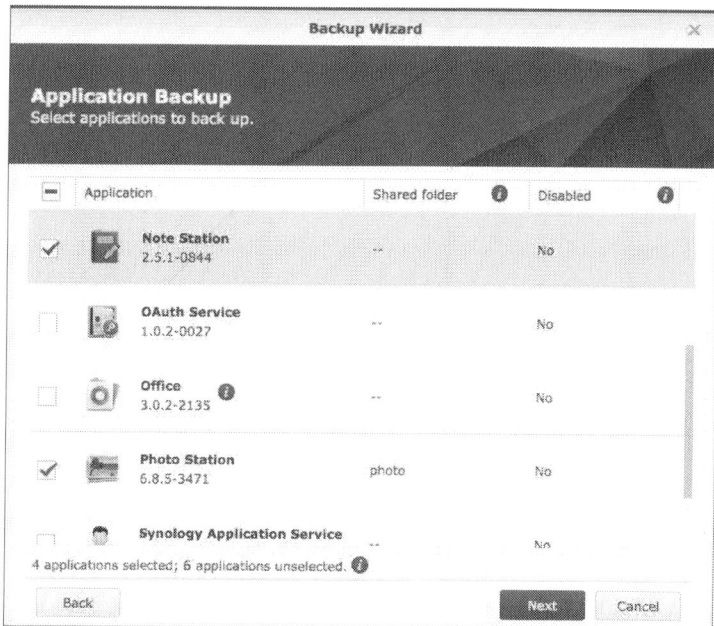

Figure 56: Select Applications to be backed up

The subsequent screen allows you to set a schedule and specify other settings. Working through it:

Change the name of the *Task* to something more descriptive, in this case we've called it *DailyBackup*.

Remove the tick from *Enable task notification* (notification requires additional setup work and can always be revisited).

Remove destination external device when backup task has successfully finished - if the backup drive is left permanently connected to the DiskStation do not tick it, but if it is removed after a backup and kept in a separate location then tick it.

Compress backup data – not particularly important either way. Compressed data takes up less space, but the backup and restore processes will be slower.

Enable backup schedule - the backup should ideally run at a time when the server is not being used or at least is not particularly busy, which will depend upon the circumstances of your household or organization. In this example the backup is set to run every weekday at 10:00pm (2200 hours) each evening.

Enable integrity check integrity – tick all the boxes to enable Hyper Backup to be able to check the integrity (accuracy and usability) of the backed-up data

Enable client-side encryption – tick to encrypt the backup. You may want to tick and specify a password if you are backing up confidential data

Having specified all the parameters, click **Next**:

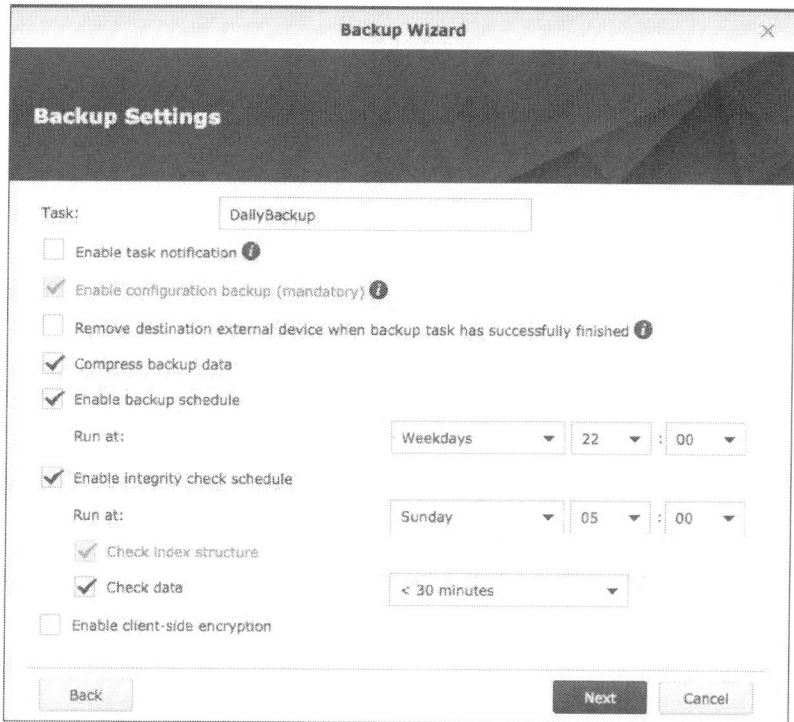

Figure 57: Backup schedule and configuration

The next screen is concerned with *Rotation Settings*. With some computer backup systems, you can keep only one backup. But suppose you are performing daily backups, have a problem and need to revert to a copy of a file made, say, a week ago – then what? With backup rotation, Hyper Backup will maintain multiple backups for as long as it can; eventually, when the backup disk is full, it will start to overwrite the oldest backups to free up the space (if you are a Mac user you may be familiar with Time Machine, which operates in a similar manner). To turn on this feature, tick the **Enable backup rotation** box followed by **Apply**. There are some optional settings, but most people will not need to worry about them as the defaults are generally fine.

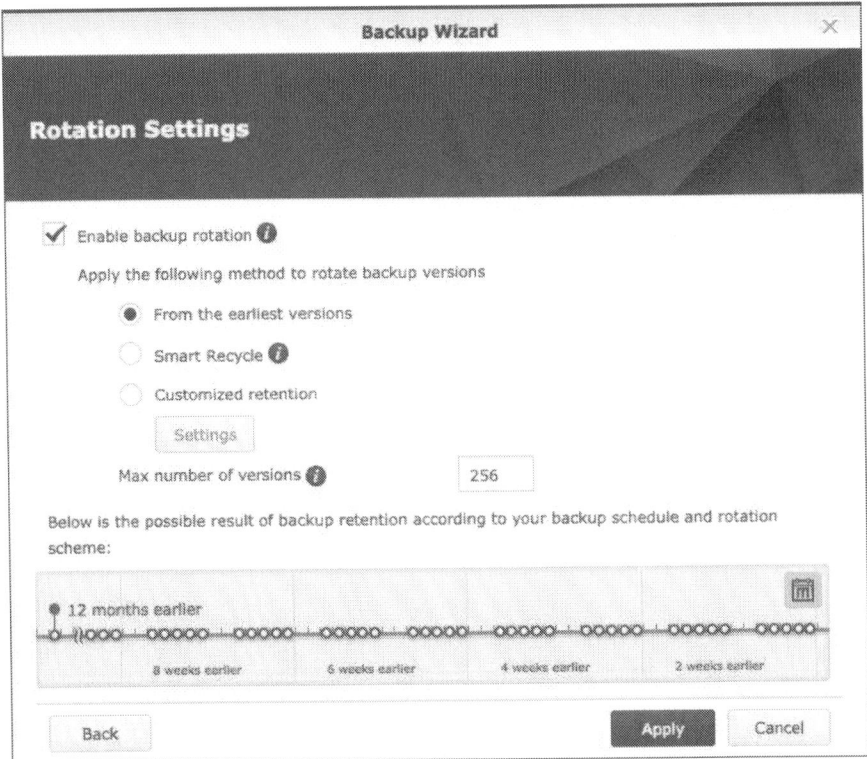

Figure 58: Rotation Settings

After clicking **Apply** you will receive a message asking whether you wish to 'Backup up now?' and it is suggested that you reply **Yes**, so as to test the newly defined backup job.

Once the backups have been setup and are working, the main Hyper Backup screen can be used to manage them. To perform a backup at any point, rather than wait for the schedule, click the **Back up now** button. To check the backup log i.e. the list of completed backups, click **Version List**. To change the parameters of the backup, click **Settings**:

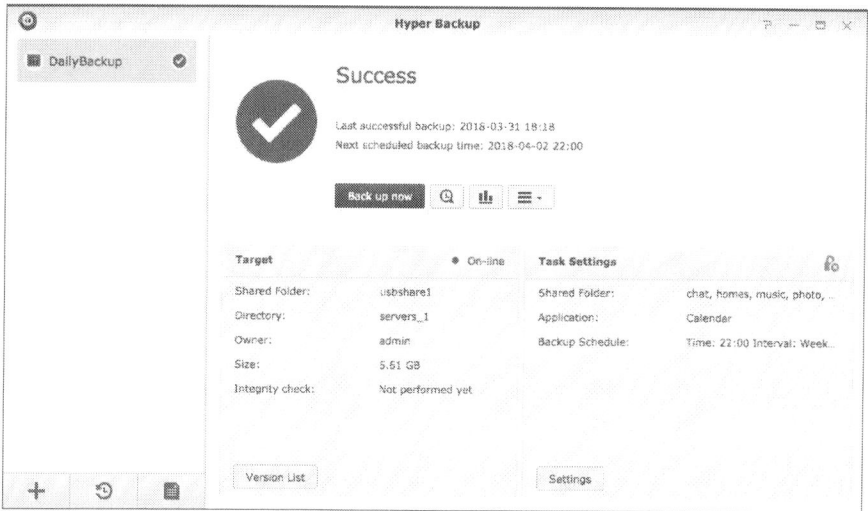

Figure 59: View backup status in main Hyper Backup screen.

One thing to note is that although the first backup may take some time – depending on how much data there is – subsequent backups should be quicker. This is because Hyper Backup uses *incremental backups*, meaning it only backs up the items that have changed since the previous backup.

To make a change to an existing backup job, click the right-hand icon followed by **Edit**. To remove an existing backup job, click **Delete**:

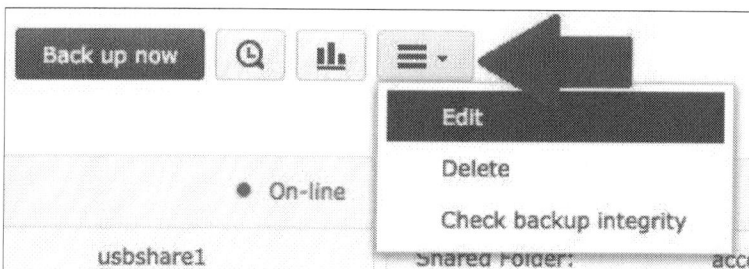

Figure 60: Modify an existing backup job

7.2 Restoring Files from a Backup

Launch Hyper Backup from the Main Menu. In the middle of the screen, next to the blue *Back up now* button, is an icon that looks like a combination watch/magnifying glass:

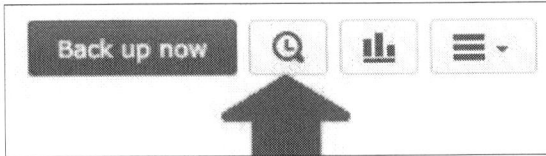

Figure 61: Icon for Backup Explorer

Click the icon to launch *Backup Explorer*:

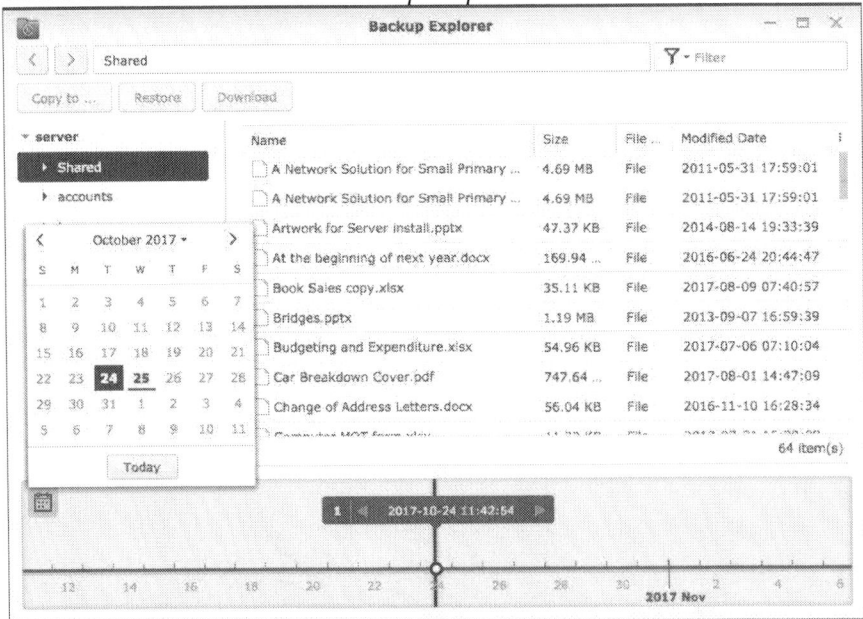

Figure 62: Backup Explorer

As the name implies, it allows you to 'explore' the backups, effectively stepping back in time until you find the one you want. The backups are displayed in a regular drive, folder, file format, exactly the same as in File Explorer. Having located the required items, you have three choices, selectable by clicking on the buttons at the top of the screen or by right-clicking on the files or folders:

Restore – the items are restored to their original location. Suppose you had deleted a file or folder; using this option you could recover it from the backup.

Copy to – the items are restored but to a different location that you choose. For instance, you might have a particular file but wish to see if an older version is more useful. By restoring to a different location, you do not have to overwrite the current one.

Download – the items are restored, but to your computer rather than to the DiskStation.

7.3 Backing Up Using Cloud Services

DiskStations can be backed up using many popular cloud services, both consumer ones such as Dropbox and Google Drive, as well as professional ones such as Microsoft Azure and S3 Storage. Synology also operate their own cloud service – C2 – which provides different tiers of storage on a paid basis, ranging from options suitable for individuals up to enterprises, with a 30-day trial available to new users. Regardless of the cloud service used, and it is possible to use multiple ones simultaneously, it is all controlled and managed using Hyper Backup.

Go to **Main Menu** and launch **Hyper Backup.** In the bottom left-hand corner of the screen click the large plus (+) sign and select **Data backup task**:

Figure 63: Choose data backup task

The *Backup Wizard* will start. Select a cloud service where you already have an account for the backup destination type, then click **Next**:

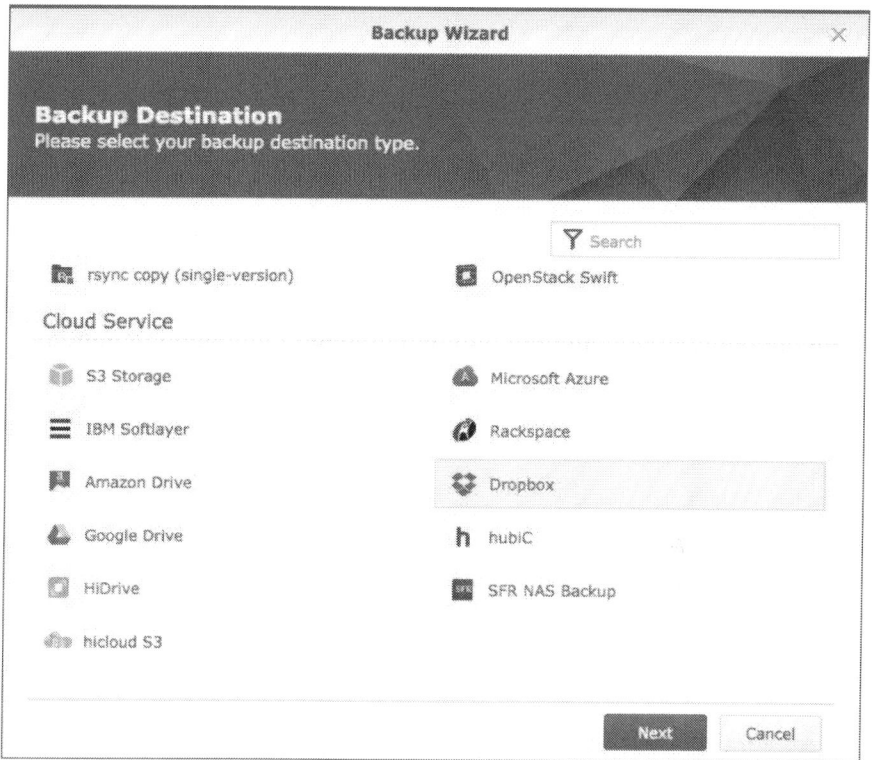

Figure 64: Choose a Cloud Service

You will be prompted to confirm that you wish to grant access to Synology Hyper Backup by the provider's website, the specifics of which will vary slightly depending on the provider. Having done so, you will be returned to the Backup Wizard to *Create backup task*; against the *Folder* dropdown, choose *Create New Folder* from the dropdown, give it a meaningful name and click **OK**:

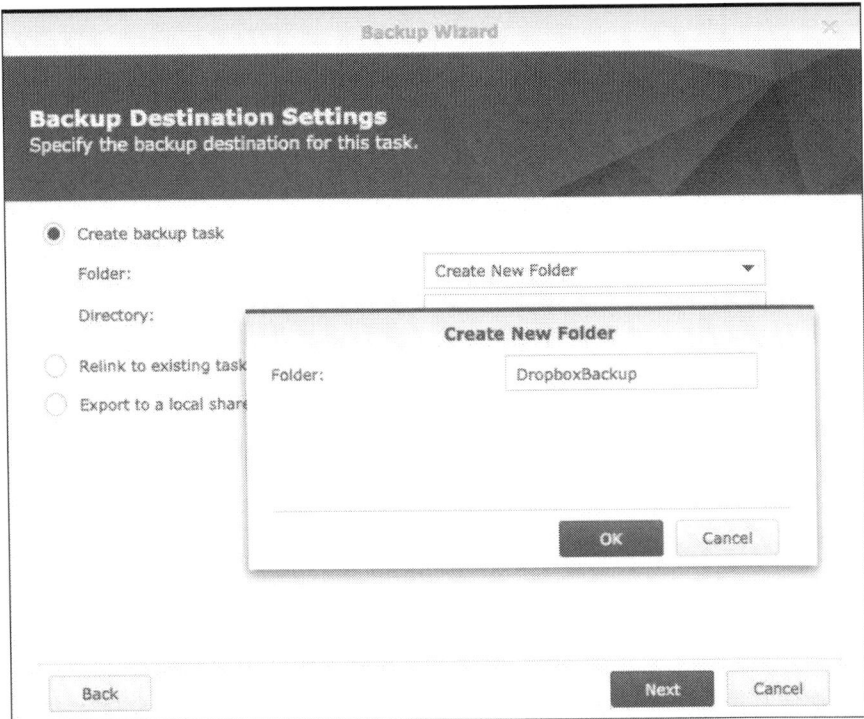

Figure 65: Create backup folder

You now need to specify a *Directory*; this could be something like *server_1*. Note that both the folder and directory refer to the cloud side and *not* the DiskStation. Click **Next.** On the subsequent screens, specify: the shared folders to be backed up; any applications to be backed up; the backup settings; rotation settings. These screens are exactly the same as when backing up to an external USB drive as described in section **7.1 Backing Up the DiskStation to an External Drive**. However, you may wish not to enable backup rotation settings, as this has storage space implications at the cloud side, plus many cloud services implement their own form of rotation or versioning (for instance, Dropbox does). Once the backup job has been defined – and there may be a short delay – you will be given the option to 'Back up now?'. It is suggested you do so in order to test it, by clicking **Yes.**

The speed of backup to a cloud service is largely dependent upon the speed of your internet connection, but is typically many times slower than a backup to a local drive. For instance, a backup of 1 terabyte that might take under an hour to a USB drive may take several days over the internet. For this reason, rather than use a cloud backup as the primary backup solution, it might be better to use it as a secondary backup for a limited selection of important data. Also note that the backup may impact on your internet connection whilst it is running, slowing down access for users and other tasks.

One important consideration is that you have sufficient space in the public cloud account. For example, a free Dropbox account only has 2GB of space (plus any additional space gained through referrals). This may be insufficient, so you may want to consider a paid account; for instance, a Dropbox Plus or Professional account. Another approach is if you have accounts with multiple providers; for instance, you could backup one folder to Dropbox, another to Google, a third to Amazon and so on. For business users with larger amounts of data, C2 may be worth exploring.

7.4 Backing up Computers to the DiskStation

If users store data on their individual computers rather than on the network, then there may be a requirement to backup that data. Synology's implication is that *Synology Drive* – discussed in the next chapter - addresses this requirement by syncing local data from the computer to the DiskStation. However, some people may not wish to use Synology Drive or use it for that particular purpose, preferring instead to use a conventional backup program. Both Windows PCs and Macs have built-in backup programs, but they have restrictions in that they only work when the computers are physically connected to the local network. Additionally, the backup program supplied with Home Editions of Windows can only backup to a local drive, such as a plug-in USB hard drive or a memory card and cannot see the network drives (shared folders) of the DiskStation. This restriction is removed by Microsoft in the more expensive Professional Editions of Windows, but Home Edition users will need to use a third party program that does have the capability, of which several are available, including free ones (an example of which is *Fbackup* from Softland). Macs users have the option of using the built-in Time Machine program, with the DiskStation taking the place of Apple's Time Capsule.

The *Cloud Station Backup* solution from Synology has the following advantages over the native Microsoft and Apple programs: it works both inside and outside the home or office, making it particularly useful for people who travel; it works with all editions and versions of Windows; the Windows, Mac and Linux versions are largely identical, making it easier to support in a mixed environment.

7.5 Cloud Station Backup

Cloud Station Backup runs on user's computers and does not require any additional software to be installed on the server, assuming: (a) you have setup QuickConnect (see **2.7 QuickConnect: The Key to Remote Connectivity**) and (b) you have already installed Drive on it (see section **6 SYNOLOGY DRIVE & OFFICE**).

Begin by downloading the Cloud Station Backup utility from the Synology website and installing it on the computer. It is available for Windows, Mac, Ubuntu (64-bit & 32-bit) and Fedora (64-bit & 32-bit). These screen shots are from the Windows version, but they all look and behave in a similar way:

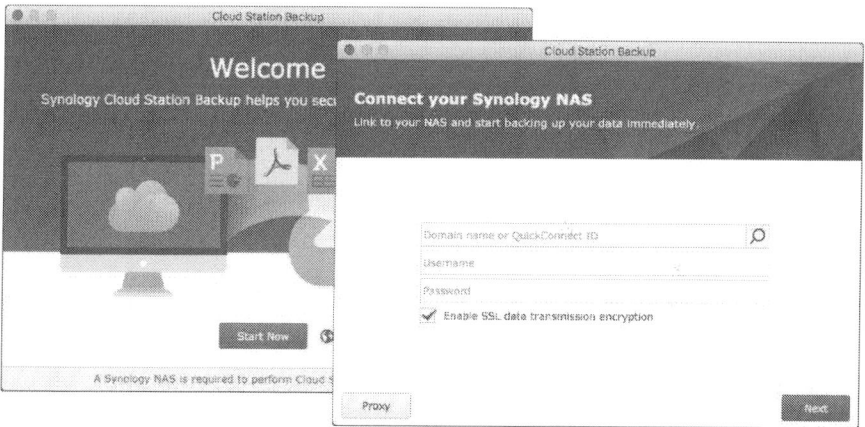

Figure 66: Enter details for QuickConnect and user

Enter the QuickConnect ID of the server, along with the user's name and password, and click **Next**. You will probably receive a warning message about the SSL certificate, which you can ignore in this instance by clicking **Proceed anyway**.

On the next screen choose the folders to be backed up. By default, the destination will be a folder called */CloudStation/Backup/name_of_computer* in the user's home folder on the server – it is possible to change this, but it is suggested that you do not do so. It is also possible to change parameters of the backup by clicking the **Backup rules** button, but the defaults will be fine for most people:

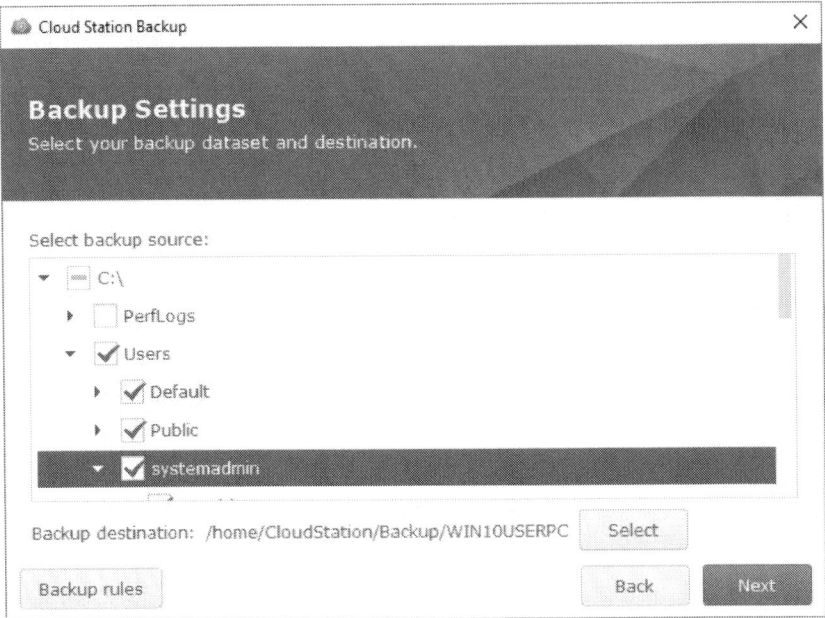

Figure 67: Choose data to backup

Upon clicking **Next**, the system will display a summary screen. Click **Done**, then **OK** to the message that is displayed:

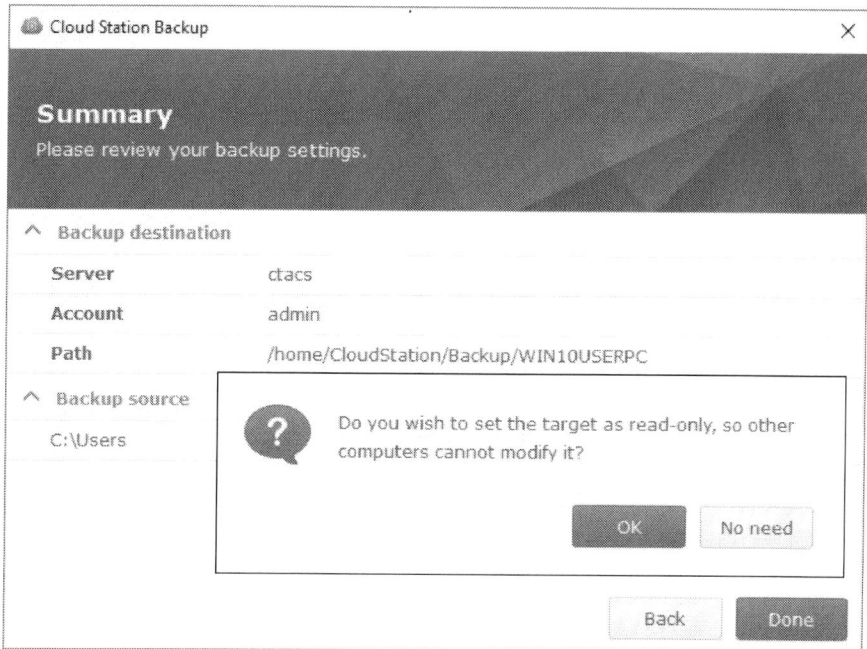

Figure 68: Summary of settings

The backup will then run and whilst it does so a status screen is displayed. Clicking on **Recent activities** will display details of the backup; to change any of the setup parameters, click **Settings**; Version Explorer allows you to work with earlier versions of the files.

Figure 69: Cloud Station Backup status screen

7.6 Backing Up Macs using Time Machine

Time Machine is the standard backup solution for Mac users, first introduced with Mac OS X 10.5. It was designed to operate with Apple's Time Capsule, a combined router/wireless access point/hard drive. However, support is provided in DSM, allowing the server to be specified as a backup destination for use by Time Machine. This is done as follows:

Create a shared folder on the server specifically for this purpose (creating shared folders is described in section **3.1 Creating a Shared Folder**). Give the folder a meaningful name e.g. *macbackup* and give **Read/Write** access to all the Mac users in the household or organization. You may also want to tick the **Hide sub-folders and files from users without permissions** box.

Next, go to **Control Panel,** choose **File Services** and click the **Advanced** tab. Scroll down to the Mac section and make sure all the **Enable Bonjour...** boxes are ticked. Click the **Set Time Machine Folders** button, tick the shared folder you just created (*macbackup* in our example) and click **Apply**:

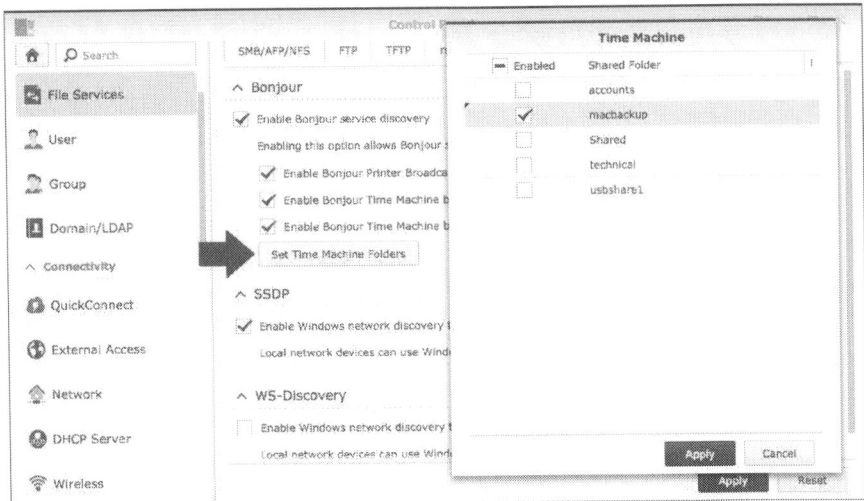

Figure 70: Settings for Time Machine in DSM

On the Mac, launch *Time Machine* (there may be some minor differences in the screenshots, depending on which version of the Mac operating system you are using). Click **Select Backup Disk** and you should be able to see the backup folder we created (*"macbackup"* in our example); highlight it and click the **Use Disk** button. It will be necessary to enter the user's name and password as previously defined on the DiskStation.

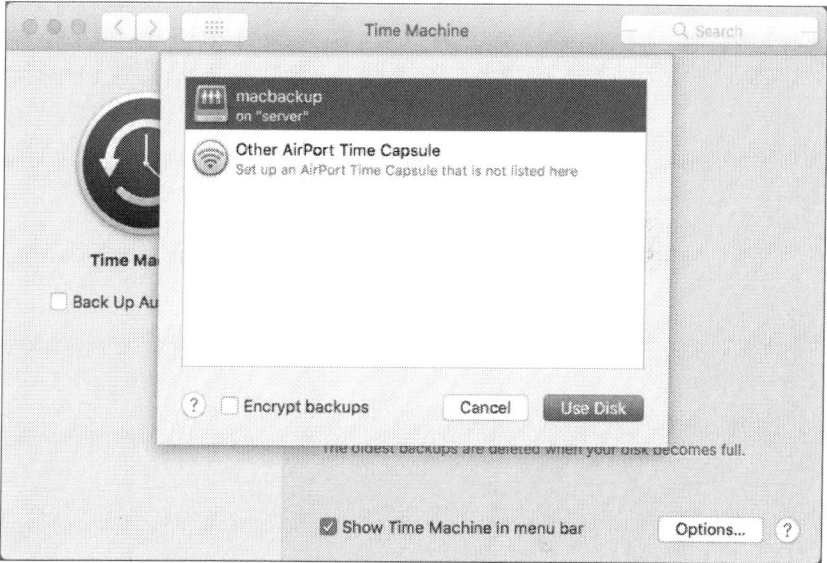

Figure 71: Select the backup folder on the server

Thereafter Time Machine behaves in a totally standard method i.e. exactly the same as though you were using Apple's own Time Capsule product.

Suggestion: to avoid the server filling up with backups, apply a quota to each Mac user. Go to **Control Panel** and click the **User** icon. Highlight a user name, click the **Edit** button, then click the **Quota** tab. In the Quota column specify a value, such as 100 GB, 250 GB or whatever value is appropriate. Click **OK**.

8 MULTIMEDIA & STREAMING

One of the most popular uses of a home network is for the storage and playback of media such as photos, music and videos. CDs and DVDs can be "ripped" into formats such as MP3 and MP4 and these copies played back from the DiskStation, thus protecting the originals against wear and tear. By maintaining a central library, the entire family can access their media from both inside and outside the household. The DiskStation is able to playback the stored media onto a variety of devices including computers, gaming consoles, tablets, smartphones, smart TVs, streaming TV devices and suitable hi-fi systems.

Note that the unauthorized copying of commercial CDs and DVDs is prohibited in most countries.

8.1 Media Server ("DLNA")

DLNA stands for *Digital Living Network Alliance*. It is a widely used standard for interconnecting home network devices in order that they can stream and play multimedia. The design goal is that DLNA devices can do so without worrying about passwords, network protocols and other technical issues. Many devices are DLNA-compliant including computers, smart televisions, media streamers, gaming boxes such as the Xbox and PS4, smartphones, Blu-ray players and more. Synology have an application – *Media Server* – which turns the DiskStation into a DLNA server.

You may have chosen to install Media Server during the initial installation of DSM, else download and install it from the Package Center. It will place an icon in the **Main Menu**. To change settings, click on the **Media Server** icon, where there are three sections that control matters: *General Settings, Browsing Settings* and *DMA Compatibility*, discussed below. However, for most people there usually isn't any need to do anything – it just works and will find any media in the *music, photo* and *video* folders that we created earlier on. Depending on how much media you have and the processing power of the DiskStation, there may be a considerable delay as Media Server indexes your files for the first time and makes them available (also see section **8.2 Media Indexing**).

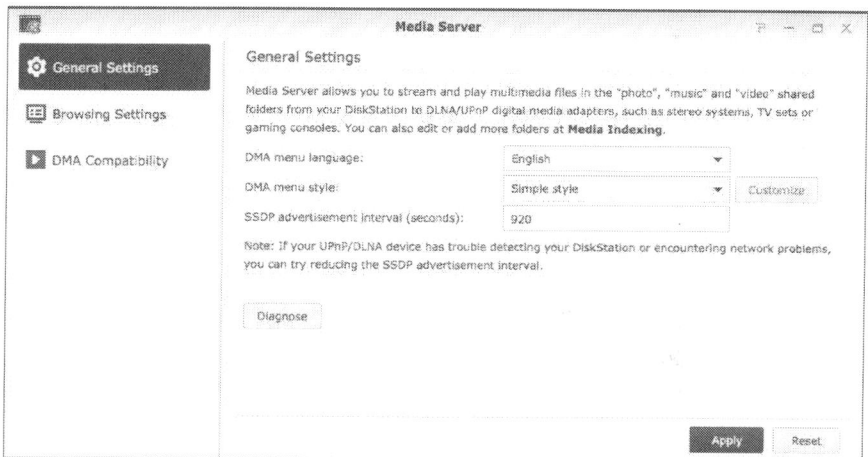

Figure 72: Main Media Server screen

At this point you should be able to connect your DLNA client to the server. As DLNA devices vary considerably there is no single method for doing so: the client may just 'see' the server, whereas on some devices it may be necessary to explicitly go into network settings or there may be an option to search for media servers. Refer to the manufacturer's instructions or website for details.

As mentioned above, Media Server just works and it is not usually necessary to change any of the settings. Having said that, there are some options that may be of relevance or interest to some people. On the Media Server screen, there are three sections:

General Settings

There are three items that can be changed:

DMA menu language – choose a language for DMA to work in. There is a choice of 20 widely used ones.

DMA menu style – the default is 'Simple style' but you could choose Advanced or iPod-style, or customize your own.

SSDP advertisement interval – the default value of 920 will be fine in nearly all cases. But occasionally, some devices, such as older smart televisions, may be DLNA-certified but have difficulties connecting to NAS-based DLNA servers. Reducing this value – try going down in steps of 100 at a time – might help.
Having made any changes, click **Apply**.

Browsing Settings

This refers to browsing for media when using DLNA client devices and how the media will appear, but is nothing to do with internet browsers. Concerned mainly with cosmetic issues, you can also enable Internet radio and integrate the Video Station database (if you are using Video Station) into Media Server.

Having made any changes, click **Apply**.

DMA Compatibility

Although it is generally assumed in this chapter that you are using MP3 for music files, other popular audio formats exist, such as *FLAC/APE, ALAC/AAC, OGG* and *AIFF*.

The Synology software can handle these formats, but not all DLNA client devices can. By ticking the **Enable audio transcoding** box, the files will be transcoded ('converted') into something that most devices can understand. Similarly, you can tick **Enable video transcoding** to do the same for *rm rmvb* and *mkv* format video files. Be aware that video transcoding uses a lot of processing power so you should not do this if you have a low-end DiskStation.

You can also restrict access to Media Server for DLNA clients in your network if, for some reason, you do not wish people to play music and such (this can be useful in some business settings, for instance).

Having made any changes, click **Apply**.

8.2 Media Indexing

If you subsequently add more photos, music and videos to the DiskStation, you may find that they do not necessarily appear in the various media applications. You can usually resolve this by re-indexing the media.

Go into **Control Panel** and choose **Indexing Service**. In the *Media Indexing* section, click the **Re-index** button:

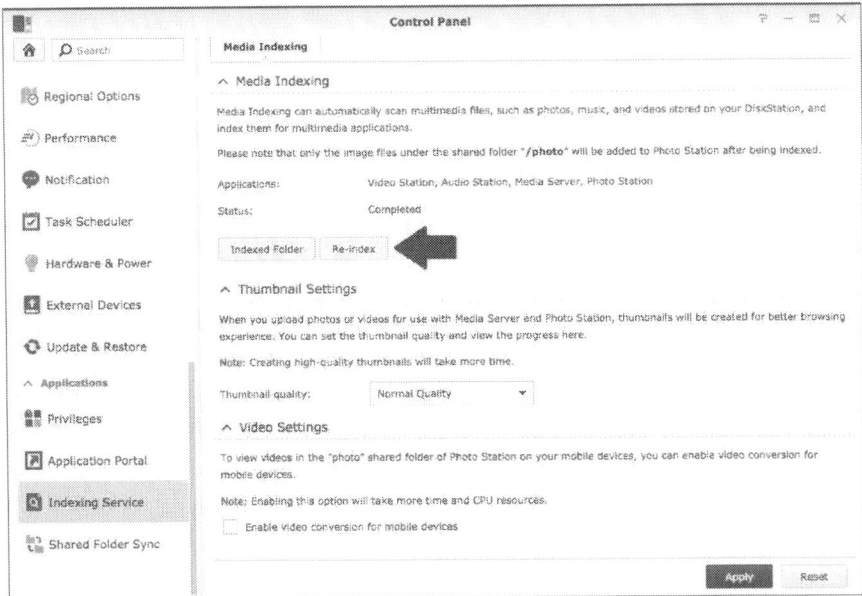

Figure 73: Media indexing

If you wish to exercise control over which folders are indexed and what media they contain, click the **Indexed Folder** button. On the resultant panel you can create, delete and edit the folders as required:

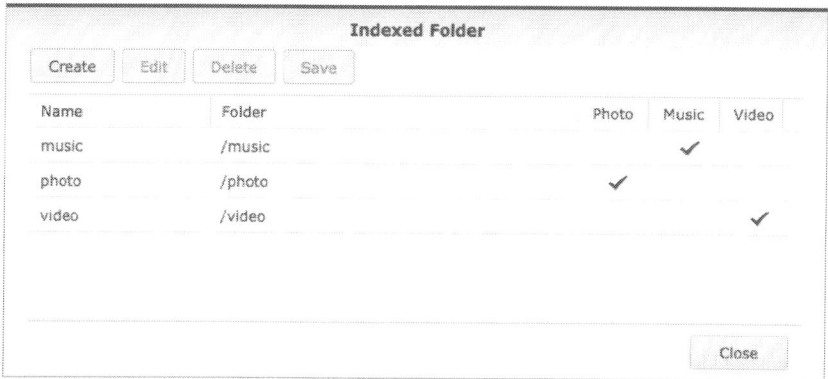

Figure 74: Choose indexed folders

There are two other sections that may be of interest:

Thumbnail Settings – thumbnails are icons that represent media files as small pictures, giving a quick preview of that file. By default, thumbnails are of *Normal Quality* but you can, if you wish, change them to *High Quality*. This might be important to, for instance, a photography business. However, it is important to appreciate that the generation of high quality thumbnails uses a lot of processing power and you probably would not wish to do this on a low-end DiskStation.

Video Settings – the videos you store on the DiskStation may be in high-resolution, suitable for viewing on a large screen television. However, such videos may be unsuitable for viewing on mobile devices, such as Smart phones (the screens are usually of lower resolution; they may have enough processing power to handle them smoothly; bandwidth may be a consideration if the device is being used outside the home or business e.g. on a 3G or 4G connection). To help with this, the DiskStation can convert videos into a lower resolution more suitable for mobile devices, which you do by ticking the **Enable video conversion for mobile devices** box. Note that this process uses a considerable amount of processing power and will work better on more powerful DiskStations.

8.3 Moments

Synology Moments is an application for managing photos and videos. It utilizes what Synology describes as a 'deep learning algorithm', enabling it to automatically sort and categorize photos with similar faces, subjects and places. Moments runs on the server, but is also designed to work with iOS and Android mobile devices. Photos taken on smartphones and tablets can be uploaded to and backed up on the DiskStation, enabling storage space to be freed up on the devices. It is thus similar in operation to products such as Apple's Photos and iCloud Photo Library or Amazon's Prime Photos, with the advantages of everything being under your own control and without ongoing subscription costs.

Begin by downloading and installing Moments from the Package Center; click the icon which is placed on the Main Menu and it will open in a new browser window. The first time it is run it will present a short tour; work through it and then click the **Start now** button, which will display the following screen:

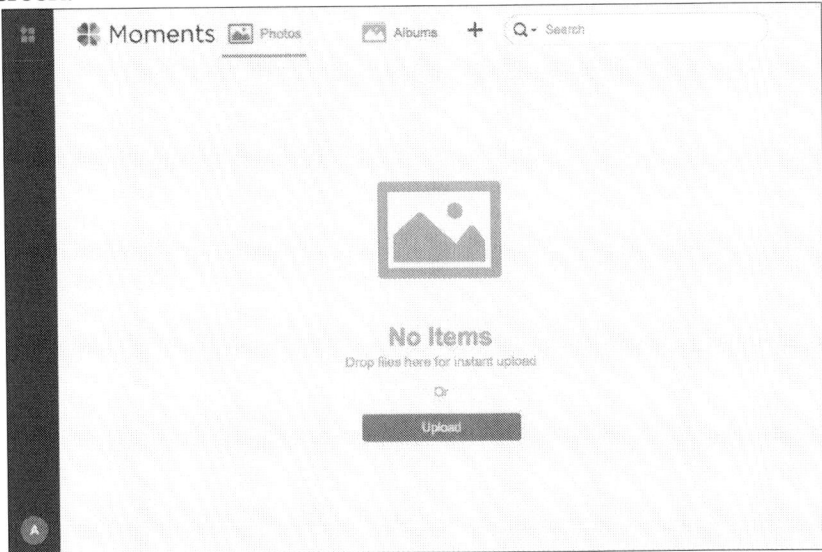

Figure 75: Initial screen in Moments

Click the **Upload** button to upload a selection of photographs, else drag them onto the app from File Manager (Windows) or Finder (Mac). Alternatively, upload them to the *home/Drive/Moments* folder if Synology Drive is being used. Depending on the number of photographs, it may a little while for Moments to process them, after which they will be displayed on the screen:

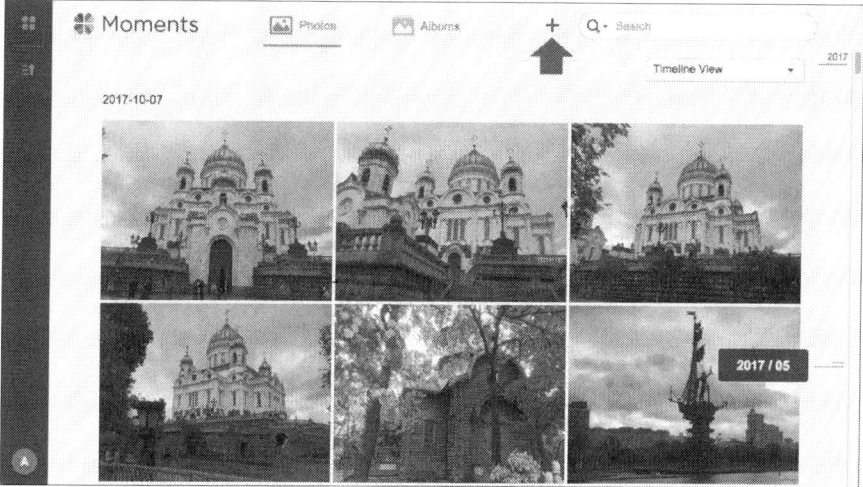

Figure 76: Photo displayed in Moments

Photos can be viewed as a timeline, or as folders. To see a photo full-screen, click it. When doing so, a number of options become available: you can scroll to the previous and next photos; share the photo with someone else; run a slideshow plus rotate or download the photo; obtain detailed information and add a tag; delete the photo; return to the main screen:

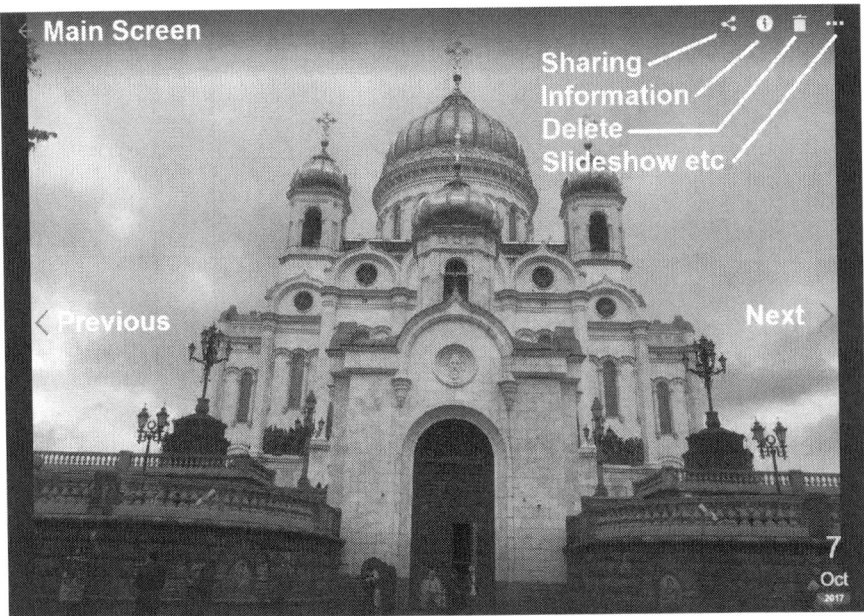

Figure 77: Viewing an individual photo

To add further images at any point, click the large plus button at the top of the main screen followed by Upload, then choose the files and folders. Having uploaded additional photos, it is then a good idea to re-index them. To do this: click on the button in the bottom left-hand corner of the main screen; select **Settings** from the pop-up menu; click on the **General** tab; click the **Re-index** button. Depending on the number of photographs, the process may take some time and you will need to review any tags, particularly the names of people who have been identified:

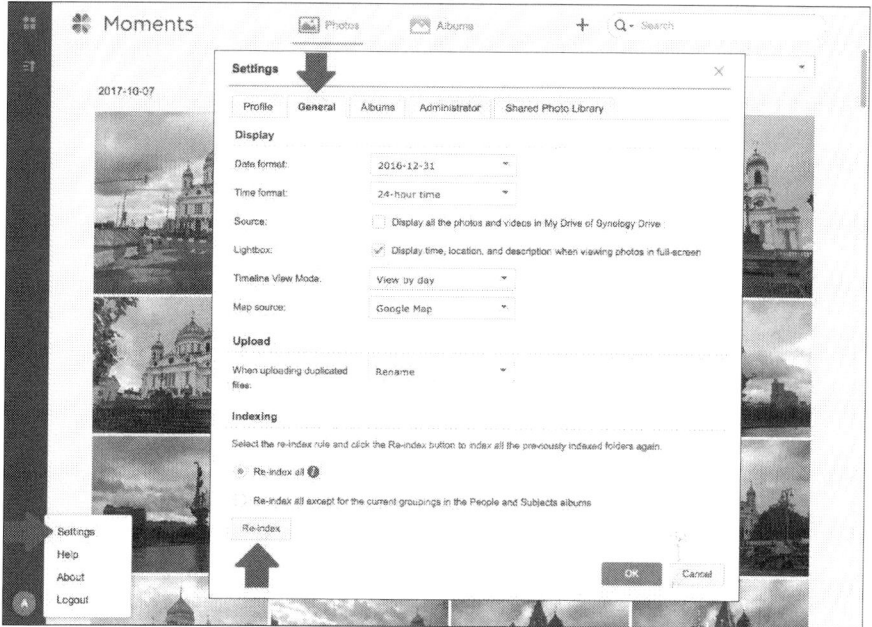

Figure 78: Settings for Indexing

Having finished with Moments, Logout using the menu in the bottom left-hand corner of the main screen.

Moments App for Smartphones

As described in the introduction, Moments is also intended for use on Smartphones and tablets and a Moments app is available from the Apple and Google stores for iOS and Android devices respectively. Having installed it, enter the QuickConnect ID for the server or it's IP address, plus a user account name and password. Slide the switch so that HTTPS is used and tap **Login**. The first time it is run the settings screen is displayed; if you want the app to backup your photos to the server so as to save storage space on the device, tap **Enable Photo Backup**. If you want to restrict uploads to Wi-Fi only, flip the switch (you may want to do this unless you have an unlimited or very generous cellular/mobile data plan):

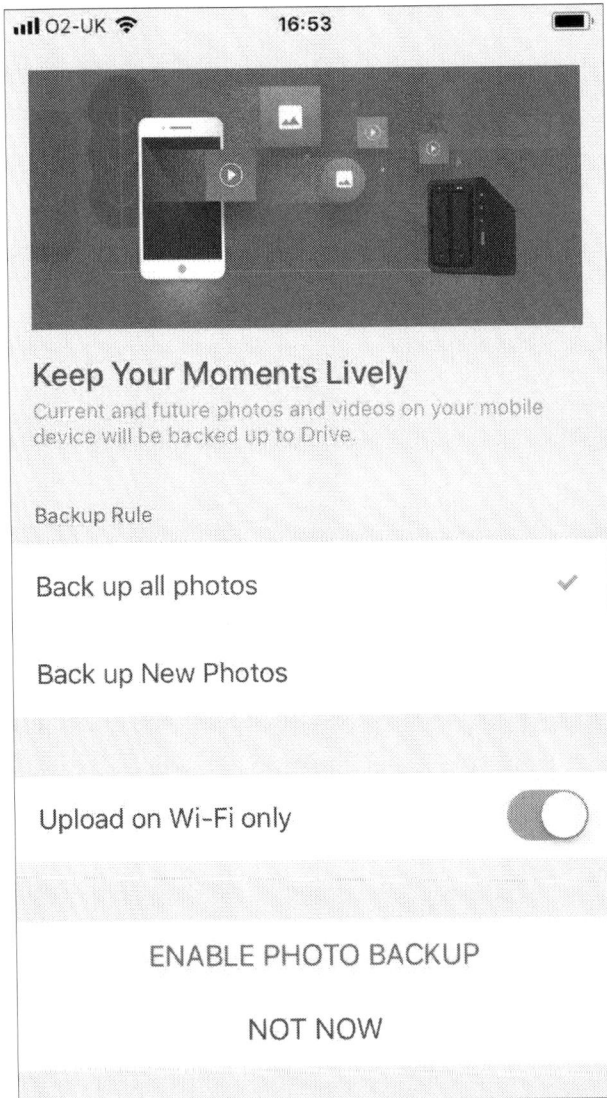

Figure 79: Settings screen in Moments App on iPhone

The main screen is similar to that of Moments on the server, with the option to change the view and to search photos based on tags. Tapping a photo causes it to display full screen, from where there are options to share, download and delete.

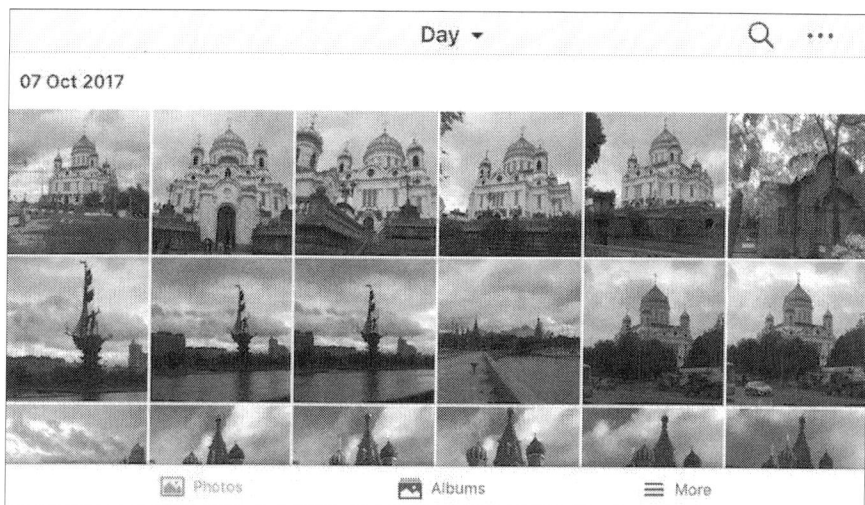

Figure 80: Main view in Moments App on iPhone

8.4 Other Synology Multimedia Applications

Synology offer a wide range of additional multimedia applications including *Audio Station, Photo Station, Video Station* and *Moments*. These are generally more capable than the Media Server discussed above and allow media to be played on a computer in the browser, or on portable devices running Android or iOS. They can be downloaded from the Package Center.

9 MISCELLANEOUS TOPICS

9.1 Package Center

Whilst the DSM operating system has a huge amount of useful functionality built-in, it is possible to extend it further through the installation of optional, mostly free, packages and this process is managed through the *Package Center*. If you installed DSM using Web Assistant, you will have been given the opportunity to download and install a useful selection of packages; some of these have already been discussed, such as *Antivirus Essential* and *Drive*, but many others are available. Many of these have been developed by Synology themselves, whilst others have been supplied by third parties. Some are business focused, others are aimed more at home users and some are applicable to both. To review what is available, click on the **Package Center** icon located on the DSM Desktop to display the following screen. Note: before using Package Center for the first time, it is necessary to accept terms and conditions and privacy statement (you may have done so during the installation of DSM).

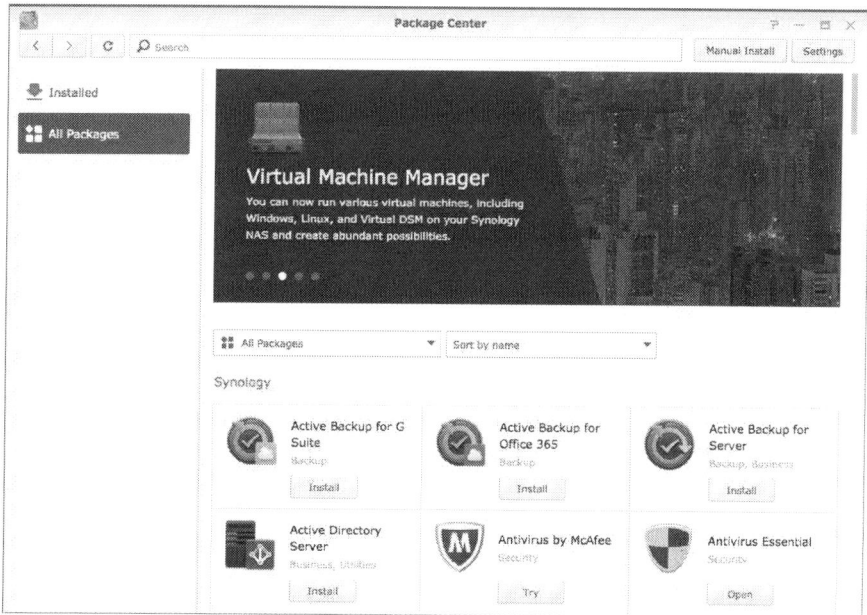

Figure 81: Package Center

At the time of writing around 130 packages are available, broken down into such categories as: *Backup; Multimedia; Business; Security; Utilities; Productivity; Developer Tools.* Not all packages are available for all DiskStations due to hardware restrictions, although the majority are and Package Center will not list ones that do not run on your model.

The following is a small selection to give a flavour of what is available:

Download Station – enables the DiskStation to manage and download BitTorrents in the background.

Surveillance Station – with this the DiskStation can control and monitor IP cameras to watch over your home or business premises and act as a NVR (Networked Video Recorder).

WordPress – enables the DiskStation to host WordPress blogs

Zafara – a compatible alternative to Microsoft Exchange that provides email, calendaring, collaborations and tasks

Mail Server – turns the DiskStation into a fully-fledged email server

MariaDB – the popular open-source relational database management system, forked from MySQL

Moodle – Virtual Learning Environment, popular in education

OpenERP – a comprehensive suite of business applications that includes Sales, CRM, Project management, Warehouse management, Manufacturing, Accounting and Human Resources

Storage Analyzer – a utility for identifying storage trends on the server and producing reports on usage, enabling you to answer questions such as: Where has all the disk space gone?

Plex Media Server – a popular media server application, used as an alternative to the standard Synology ones.

To download and install a package, click on its **Install** button. If you have more than one volume in your system, choose which volume it will be installed on. It is suggested that all apps are installed onto a single volume for consistency. Some apps have dependencies, which will result in other components and apps being automatically downloaded and installed alongside them; this is quite normal and nothing to be concerned about. The Package Center provides all the mechanisms necessary for downloading, installing, managing, updating and removing apps. Clicking on an installed package within the Package Center will show an Action drop-down where the package can be Stopped, Uninstalled and set to Auto-update:

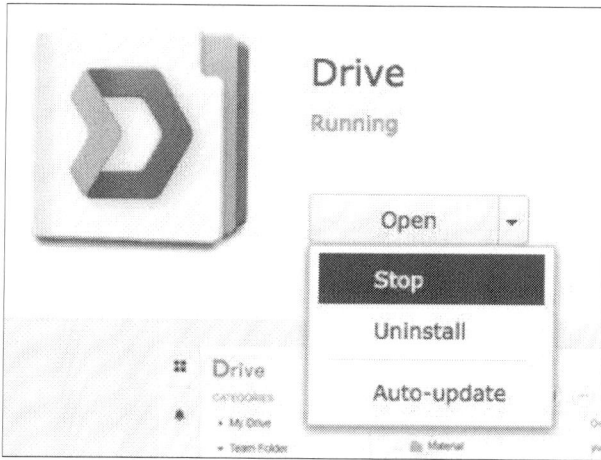

Figure 82: Controlling an installed package

9.2 Security Advisor

Security Advisor is the starting point for DSM security. It provides an 'at a glance' assessment of the areas in which the DiskStation may be vulnerable. It is located in the **Main Menu** and is run by clicking on its icon. It is good practice to run it on a regular basis e.g. once a month.

The first time Security Advisor is run it asks whether the DiskStation is being run in a home or business environment, as the security requirements and recommendations are slightly different between them (in simplistic terms the business option is more demanding). Make a choice and click **Start**. The Security Advisor will run for a short while and then display a screen of its findings, along with any recommendations:

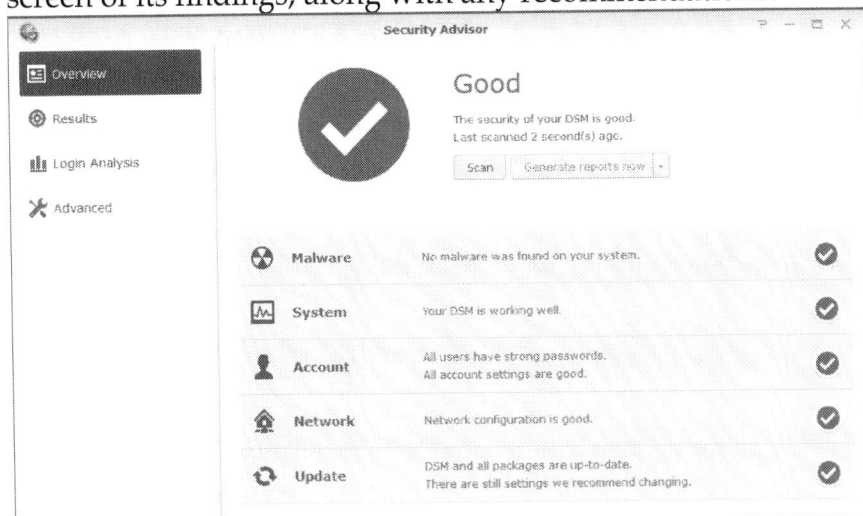

Figure 83: Results and recommendations from Security Advisor

There are five topics considered: *Malware, System, Account, Network* and *Update* – and they are helpfully traffic-lighted as: *Red* (a problem needs to be addressed); *Amber* (warning – something needs looking at); *Green* (everything is okay). One or more messages may be listed against a topic and clicking on them will display additional information, such as a suggested course of action, which should be followed through.

9.3 Antivirus Essential

The chances of a DiskStation becoming infected with a virus are low as DSM is based on a customized version of Linux and as such is not particularly susceptible. However, the files being stored on it by Windows computers and other clients may be infected and these are what need to be checked to prevent further distribution. Synology's *Antivirus Essential* is a free download from the Package Center and runs on the DiskStation itself. However, do note that separate provision still needs to be made for the workstations (e.g. Microsoft Defender, AVG, McAfee etc. for Windows PCs) as there is no linkage between them and the server, nor is this intended as a replacement for security software on desktops and laptops.

Having downloaded and installed Antivirus Essential from the Package Center, an icon will appear in the Main Menu - click it to display the console. Three types of on-demand scan are available and it is fairly self-evident what each does. By default, the latest anti-virus signatures will be downloaded before the scan commences, although this behaviour can be changed from the **Settings** option. You can also click **Update** at any time:

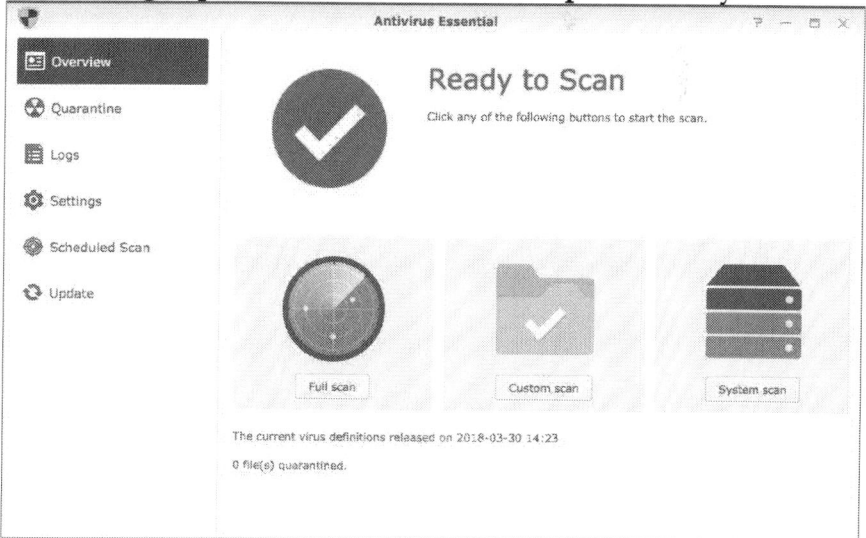

Figure 84: Antivirus Essential main screen

Scanning can result in high CPU and memory utilization, particularly on DiskStations with less than 512MB RAM and, depending on the amount of data stored on the DiskStation, can be time consuming. For this reason, it is best done as a scheduled task out of hours, for instance during the middle of the night or at the weekend. To schedule a scan, click on the **Scheduled Scan** option followed by the **Create** button. In this example, the DiskStation is set to do a full scan on a Sunday morning, starting at midnight:

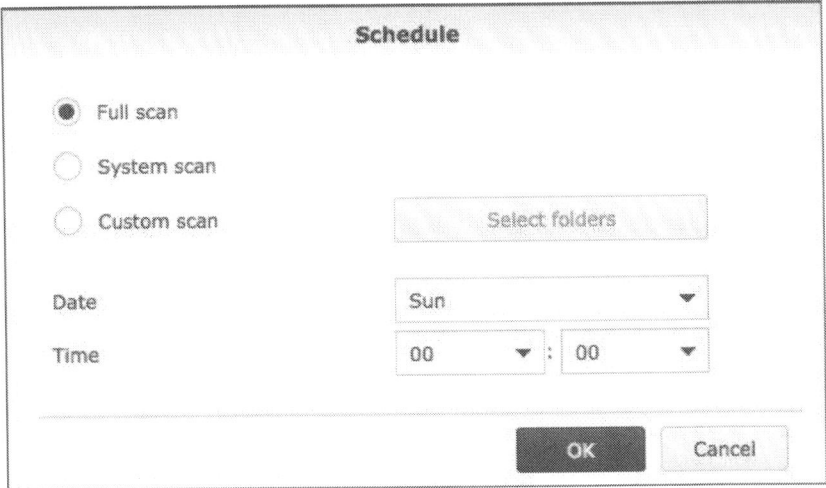

Figure 85: Scheduling a scan

The results of scans and other activities pertaining to the app are recorded in log files. These can be found by clicking on the **Logs** option.

9.4 Password Settings

When a user account is created on the DiskStation a password has to be specified. Passwords should be non-obvious – under no circumstances should words such as 'password', 'secret', 'diskstation', 'synology', 'admin' and so on be used as these are easily guessed. Nor is it a good idea to have the password the same as the user's name or a close variant thereof. The best passwords combine a mixture of upper and lower letters, numbers and punctuation and are not too short in length. For instance, a password such as *!N3y!YoRk!* would be quite difficult for someone to guess. By default, DSM requires passwords of at least six characters in length, but can be configured to enforce "stronger" passwords. A judgement has to be made regarding how strong the passwords should be; by way of guidance, businesses generally require stronger passwords than home systems and if the server is accessed remotely then the passwords should be as strong as possible.

To make changes, go to **Control Panel** and click the **User** icon. Click the **Advanced** tab to display the following panel and expand the *Password Settings* section:

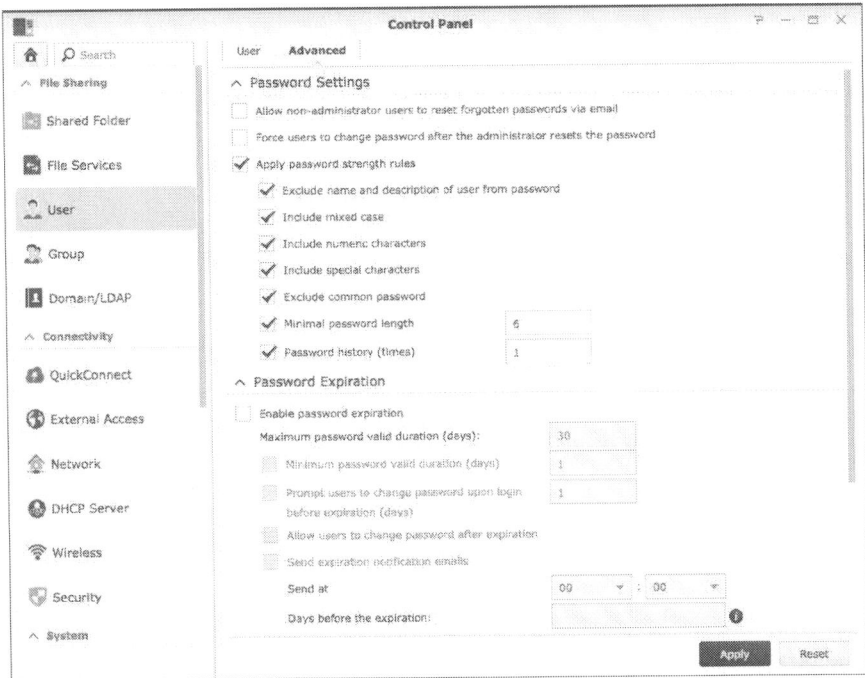

Figure 86: Password Settings and Password Expiration

Tick the **Apply password strength rules box** and tick the conditions to apply. In the above example: the user name cannot be part of the password; a mixture of upper and lower case letters have to be used, along with numbers and special characters (punctuation); the password must be at least 8 characters long; the user cannot use the same password again. Click **Apply** to make the changes.

It is also possible to enable automatic password expiration. For instance, passwords can be set to expire every 30 days and/or the users prompted to change their password at that time. Having passwords that expire in this manner is considered good practice from a security standpoint, especially in businesses.

Note that these settings will apply to all users of the system.

9.5 Manually Checking the DiskStation Using Widgets

Widgets are small panels available to the Admin user that provide status information, most of which relate to the health of the system. Click on the icon in the top right-hand corner of the screen; the resultant panel can be customized by clicking the plus sign in the top left-hand corner. There is a selection of items that can be displayed and the number that can be shown at once depends upon the resolution of the screen and size of the browser window. A good selection would be: *System Health, Resource Monitor* and *Storage,* for instance.

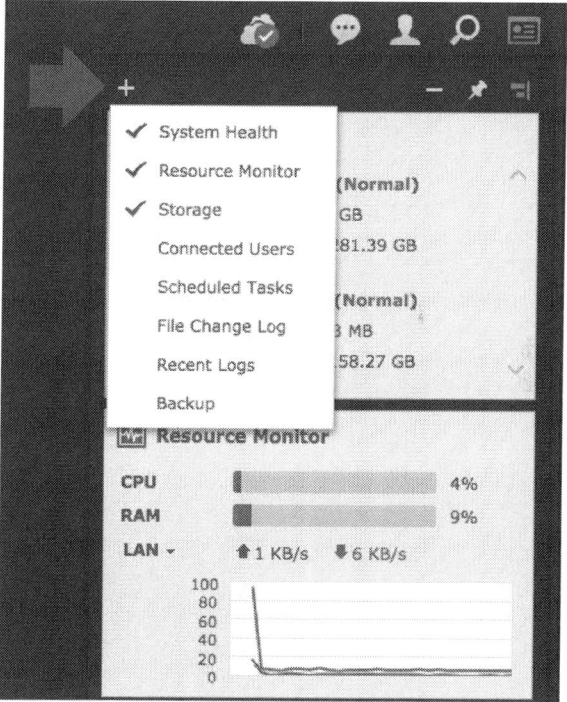

Figure 87: Setting up Widgets to check server status

The panel can be dragged anywhere convenient on screen. To put it away, click again on the icon in the top right-hand corner of the screen.

9.6 Checking the Health of the Disks

It is a good idea to check the health of the hard drives in the DiskStation on a regular basis, especially if there appear to be problems or if the DiskStation has shut down unexpectedly for any reason. This can be done manually or can be scheduled to take place automatically.

To check manually, go to the **Main Menu** and start **Storage Manager**. On the left-hand side of the screen click **HDD/SSD**. On the **HDD/SSD** tab, highlight the disk drive to be tested and click the **Health Info** button, then the **S.M.A.R.T. Test** tab. A *Quick Test* or *Extended Test* can be performed; the former is a lot quicker and generally speaking is sufficient in most circumstances. The time taken for the test depends upon the number and capacity of the drives but is usually several minutes. If a drive fails the S.M.A.R.T. test then it should be replaced at the earliest opportunity:

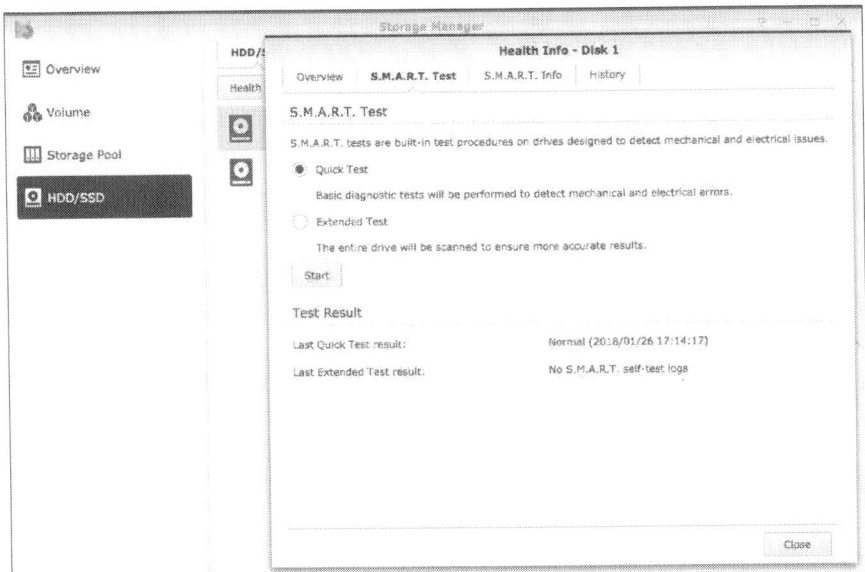

Figure 88: S.M.A.R.T. test for hard drives

To automate the testing, click on the **Test Scheduler** tab within the **HDD/SSD** page of **Storage Manager**. Depending on the options chosen during the initial installation of DSM, you may find that there is already a test schedule in place. Otherwise, click the **Create** button. Give the task a meaningful name e.g. *Test Drives* and select **Quick Test** and **Test all disks**. Click the **Schedule** tab. Setup a suitable schedule (e.g. run every monthly in the example below) then click **OK**.

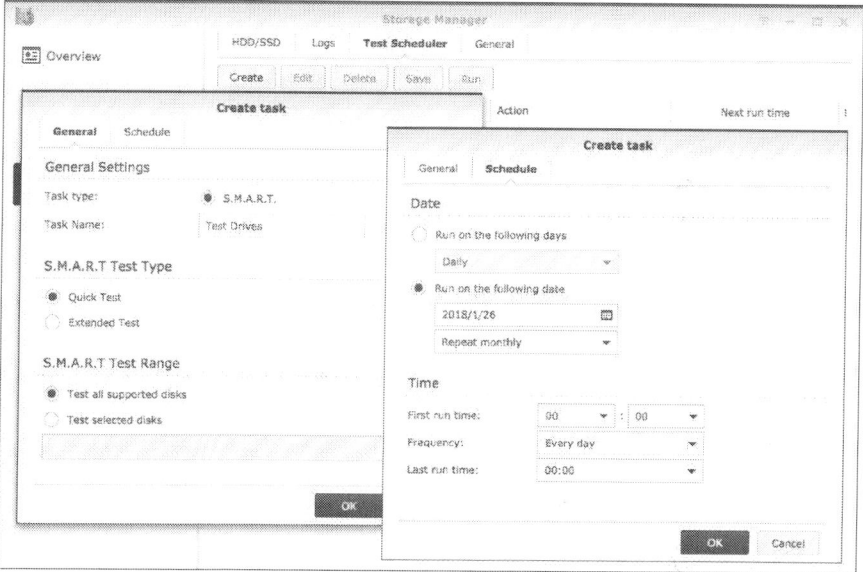

Figure 89: Setting up a schedule to test the hard drives

9.7 Checking for DSM Updates

The DSM software is updated on a regular basis by Synology. Updates may be major e.g. from DSM 6 to DSM 7, although typically these only occur every couple of years. Significant updates e.g. from DSM 6.2 to DSM 6.3 are more frequent, typically every 9-12 months. Additionally, there are more rapid updates to fix problems and these are made available by Synology as necessary; as these are often in response to specific security threats it is important that they are applied in a timely manner.

If an update is available, it will be indicated by the appearance of the digit for number one on the Control Panel icon. Alternatively, to check for updates at any point, launch **Control Panel** and click the **Update & Restore** icon. To check if an update is of relevance, click on the **What's New** link and follow the various Synology forums available on the internet. If the update is required, click the **Download** button. Once the download is complete, the button will change to read **Update Now**. As updates invariably require a reboot of the system, it is suggested that they are done at a time outside of normal working hours. Also, the server data and configuration information should be backed up before installing an update:

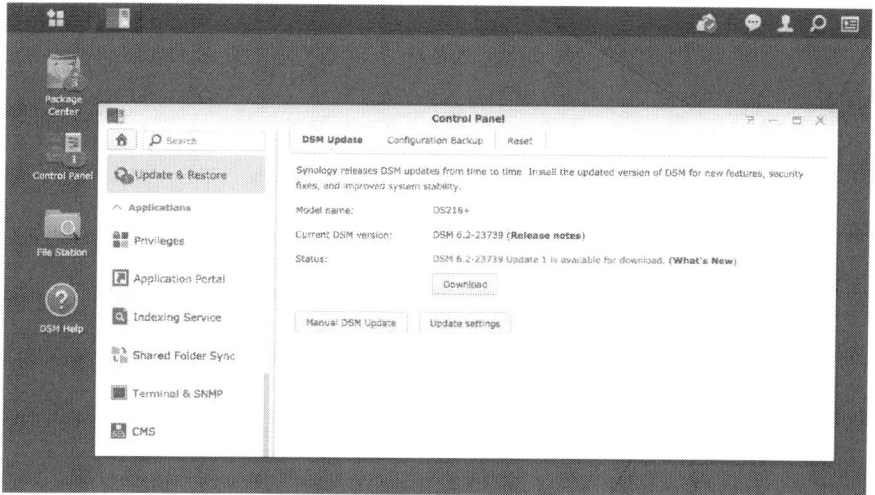

Figure 90: DSM update available

The settings for DSM updates can be changed by clicking the **Update settings** button. Whilst keeping DSM up-to-date is recommended for most installations, a more cautious approach to updating may be followed, particularly in a business environment. In such cases, the best option might be to check for **Important updates only**.

9.8 Support Center

The *Support Center* is found in the Main Menu and enables you to contact Synology directly for support and assistance should you have problems that you cannot resolve yourself. There are two tabs: the first – *Contact Support* - is for sending a message to Synology Support; the second – *Support Services* - is for setting up remote access so that Synology can take control of the DiskStation in order to gather information or apply changes. This is not left permanently enabled, rather you would tick the **Enable remote access** box when specifically requested to by Synology and then provide them with the unique *Support identification key* that is generated at the time. You can specify which items can be accessed. Having made the changes, click **Apply**.

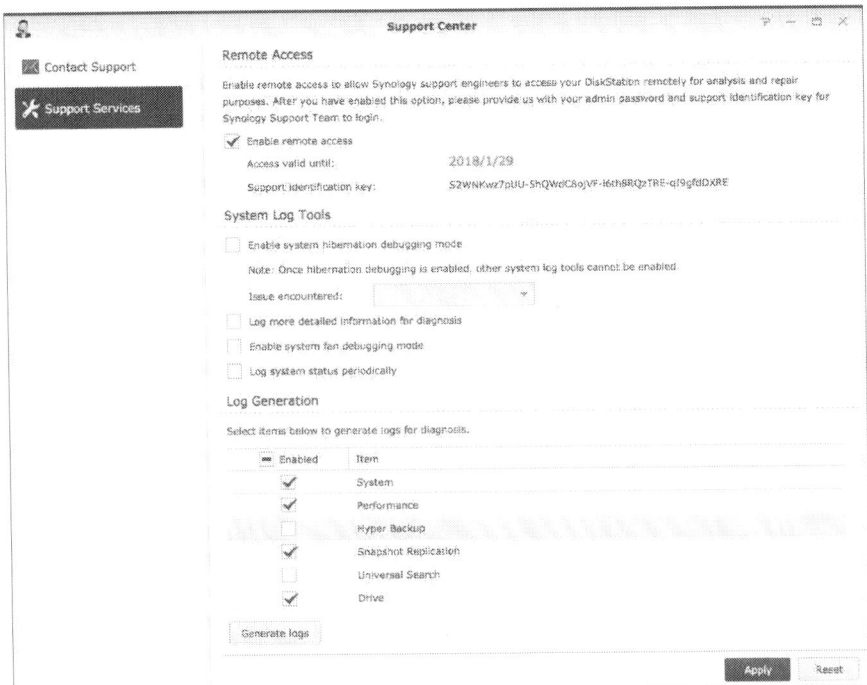

Figure 91: Support Center screen

9.9 Printing

One advantage of networking is that it allows printers to be shared, thus potentially saving money as well as physical space. There are three methods for sharing a printer on the network:

USB through DSM – Most USB-only printers can be plugged directly into the DiskStation, with DSM handling the sharing.

Ethernet or wireless through DSM – The printer is connected to the network and DSM handles the sharing.

Ethernet or wireless but independent – Most modern printers have built-in Ethernet or wireless connections, giving them an existence on the network totally independent of any server or computers.

The first technique – sharing USB printers - would once have been considered a Big Thing. These days most new printers have built-in Ethernet or wireless connections, meaning it is no longer the killer feature that it once was. The second technique is analogous to the way network printers have traditionally worked; print jobs are first sent to the server, which then feeds them out ("spools them") to the printer. This has some advantages in terms of control in a larger business environment with many users and printers, but is usually inappropriate in a household or small business. The third category of printers – ones with built-in network connections - are intelligent devices in their own right and can talk directly to computers independently without a server acting as a middleman and are the best ones to use. In the case of such printers the DiskStation has no significance at all and you simply follow the manufacturer's normal installation procedure on each of your computers.

The exact method for setting up any particular printer varies, but the following principles can usefully be followed:

Printers typically have wireless and/or wired connections. Wired connections are preferable although by no means essential, as performance is usually better compared to wireless.

Configure the printer with a fixed or static IP address. This should be adjacent to the address of the server and away from the address range used by the computers. Suppose, for instance, that the internet gateway is 192.168.1.1 and the server is 192.168.1.2. If two printers were added to the network, then suitable addresses would be 192.168.1.3 and 192.168.1.4. The simplest way to set the IP address is on the printer itself; alternatively, the technique of a reserving an IP address on the DHCP server (commonly the router in a home or small business setup) can be used.

Download the latest drivers for the printers. Consider storing the drivers on the DiskStation so that they can then be copied to the individual computers, rather than have to download them from the internet each time. The *technical* folder is a good location for this.

Printer manufacturers sometimes offer a choice of drivers, for instance a basic one as well as a full-featured one. Use the basic one, as the full-feature ones sometimes have superfluous features designed to capture marketing information and sell you more cartridges. However, be aware that with some multifunction devices (combined printers/copiers/scanners) not all functions may be available in a networked environment, or may require additional software from the manufacturer to fully utilise them.

9.10 Personalizing the Desktop

Each user of the system can personalize their individual desktop or view of DSM. Characteristics that can be customized include: Wallpaper; Choice of desktop icons; Main Menu style; Language. To change items, the user should click the **Options** icon in the top right-hand corner of the screen – it looks like the head and shoulders of a person - and choose **Personal** from the drop-down menu.

Wallpaper

Click the **Desktop** tab. Tick the **Customize color** and **Customize wallpaper** boxes to change the colour of the screen or choose a wallpaper by clicking **Select image**; there are several built-in ones or add an image of your own by navigating the list of folders. If you use your own images they should be JPG/JPEG format and no larger than about 1-2 MB.

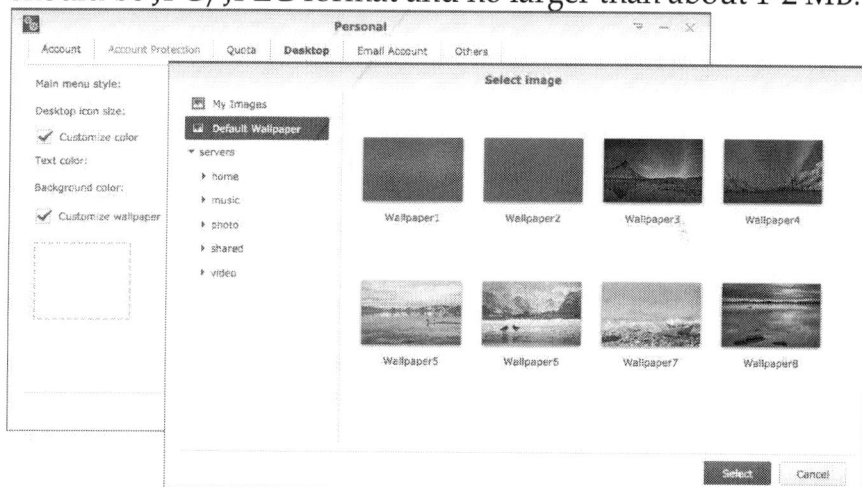

Figure 92: Desktop wallpapers

Desktop Icons

When viewing the Main Menu or the Control Panel, simply drag an icon from it towards the left-hand side of the screen and a copy will be placed on the Desktop. To remove an icon from the Desktop, right-click it and click **Remove Shortcut**.

Main Menu Style

The Main Menu can be viewed full-screen or as a drop-down in the top left-hand corner of the screen. Within the **Desktop** tab, click on the *Main menu style* field and make a choice.

Language

A user can work with DSM in the language of their choice, regardless of whatever language the server is configured in. This can be very useful in environments where multiple languages are used, such as English and Spanish in parts of the United States, or French and English in Canada. To switch language, click the **Account** tab and use the *Display language* drop-down. The languages currently supported are: Danish; German; English; Spanish; French; Italian; Hungarian; Dutch; Norwegian; Polish; Portuguese and Brazilian Portuguese; Swedish; Turkish; Czech; Russian; Japanese; Korean; Simplified and Traditional Chinese.

9.11 Resetting the Admin Password if Lost

In the event that the *admin* password is lost or forgotten, it is relatively simple to reset it. On the DiskStation is a reset button, usually on the back of the unit. Whilst the system is running, insert a very small screwdriver or a paperclip into the reset hole and press gently for about 5 seconds until the unit makes a loud beep. This will reset the *admin* password to the default value, which is a blank (i.e. no password). Log into the server immediately and assign a new password.

The ease with which this can be done means that it is important to protect the server, particularly in a business environment. Best practice is that the unit is located out of sight and reach, for instance in a cupboard or a locked room or generally out of reach.

9.12 Preparing the DiskStation for Disposal

If the DiskStation is to be disposed of, first make sure that backups of all important data have been taken, using the techniques described in section **7 BACKUPS**.

From the **Control Panel** choose **Update & Restore**. Click the **Reset** tab and on it click the **Erase All Data** button. A warning message is displayed; if you have changed your mind click **No** now else tick the box and click the **Erase All Data** button. You will be prompted to enter the admin password - the DiskStation will be restored to the initial factory state and the data on the disk(s) deleted, after which it will be rebooted.

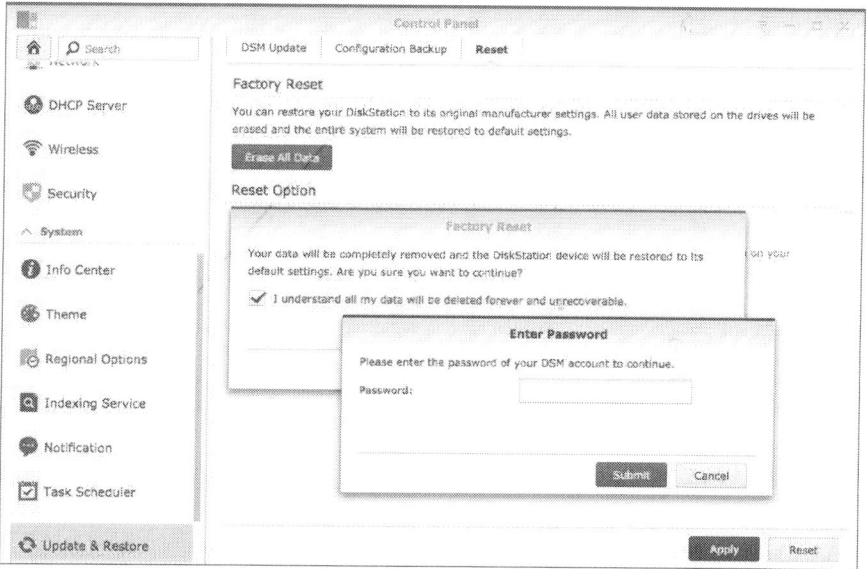

Figure 93: Factory reset

Thank you!

We hope that you have found this guide helpful and interesting.

We pride ourselves on the accuracy of our guides and they are reviewed and updated several times a year. However, as the DSM software and utilities are regularly updated it is possible that very recent changes may not be reflected. If you have any suggestions or have found errors or areas for improvement, please let us know at *enquiry@ctacs.co.uk*. Please quote the date that is stated at the beginning of page 2 so we know what edition you have. Thank you.

37747049R00081

Printed in Great Britain
by Amazon